CROSBY
CURIOSITIES

CROSBY
CURIOSITIES

MICHAEL STAMMERS

TEMPUS

Frontispiece: An attractive ship wind vane at Beach Lawn, Waterloo.

First published 2006

Tempus Publishing Limited
The Mill, Brimscombe Port,
Stroud, Gloucestershire, GL5 2QG
www.tempus-publishing.com

© Michael Stammers, 2006

British Library Cataloguing in Publication Data.
A catalogue record for this book is available from the British Library.

ISBN 0 7524 3864 6

Typesetting and origination by Tempus Publishing Limited.
Printed in Great Britain.

CONTENTS

Acknowledgements

Many people have helped with information. I must mention the staff of the Crosby Local History Library, the Merseyside Sites and Monuments Record, Frank Large, Roger Hull, John Quirk, Joseph Sharples of Liverpool University and all the other people who supplied information about their homes, families or businesses. Most of the photographs I have taken for this book myself. But the pictures of the Celtic head and the figurehead of the *Rosebud* were supplied by National Museums Liverpool. Most of the old advertisements come from the local directories in the Local History section of Crosby Library.

Introduction

Crosby is a suburb of Liverpool, administered by the Metropolitan Borough of Sefton, but it has a great sense of its own identity and when locals talk about Crosby Village, they are right. There are wide ranging social networks evolved from time at school or through organisations or family ties. There are institutions which have a distinct Crosby identity. These include the local newspaper, the *Crosby Herald*, the local football and rugby teams and institutions such as the Merchant Taylors' School, the Crow's Nest or the Crosby Gilbert and Sullivan Society.

Most of its area is covered by roads and houses, but it was not always like that. It was once a sandy stretch of the Lancashire coast with a few scattered farmsteads and a small centre around the village green at the junction of Moor Lane and Little Crosby Road. Most of its history is relatively recent. It did not become a parish separate from the ancient mother church at Sefton until 1853. The popularity of sea bathing from the end of the nineteenth century saw the rise of separate resorts of Waterloo and Seaforth, and the establishment of a rail link to Liverpool made it possible for large numbers of better-off people to live in Crosby and go to work in Liverpool. And this is still very much Crosby's role today. It is a commuter area probably with as many people taking the car to work as go by train or bus. It never had great industries, but it had thriving small businesses which supplied local needs and many still survive in spite of the competition from supermarkets. There may be no family grocers, but there are still plenty of corner shops, and many new businesses ranging from sun-tanning salons to cafes and dress shops.

My purpose in writing this book is to explore what remains of Crosby's past on the ground. In other words, what you could see here and now. My approach is to tell the story of Crosby so far as possible through what is here today. This means tangible survivals such as the early nineteenth-century seafront terraces of Waterloo or the letterhead of Thorougoods brewery. Sometimes it means moving outside Crosby in search of such relics or comparable things which no longer exist in Crosby itself. They are what I mean by 'curiosities' – things that intrigue and have a story to tell. This also includes things that you may not have noticed. There is a wealth of material that could be used. Every house has a story because of the various families who have lived in it over the years. It is not possible to include every house or even every street. My choice of examples is personal and the main focus has tended to be on Great Crosby and Waterloo. But Seaforth and Hightown, which were part of the original parish, will be included along with Little Crosby, the home of the Blundells, the local landowners, and Sefton with the mother church of the whole area, St Helen's.

I have divided the book into two parts. Part one is a general commentary on different aspects of Crosby's development from the shore to local institutions, and part two covers the different types of building materials found in Crosby plus a final chapter on signs, dates and inscriptions. I have also deliberately not chosen pictures of the most prominent or well-known buildings. This is because they have been covered by other books such as the pictorial histories recently compiled by Tom Heath, the local historians of Sefton Libraries and John Cochrane's *History of Great Crosby*. There is a full bibliography at the end of the book which gives the references for these and other useful books and articles.

Part One

Some Aspects of the Development of Crosby

This first section is devoted to some of the main aspects of the Crosby district's physical development and relating them to wider national changes. There is an emphasis on the tangible evidence of the changes, starting with shore and the land itself. Most of the original landscape of dunes, marshes and woodlands has been lost to more recent developments. Nevertheless extensive research along the whole Sefton coast and the Crosby shore shows that this area has always been part of a long-term process of change, including rising sea levels and dune formation.

Tangible evidence for early human settlements is scarce, and some of the few finds that have been made were destroyed in the bombing of Liverpool Museum in 1941. More recent fieldwork and aerial photography has revealed previously hidden sites such as a Romano-British farmstead. Place names also reveal a mixture of settlers in the post-Roman era.

Evidence from records as opposed to archaeological finds begins in the later Middle Ages and portrays a small farming community. This was able to support its own chapel of ease by the sixteenth century yet still had to bury its dead at the mother church of St Helen's, Sefton until 1853. Henry VIII's split with Rome and the enforcement of a state-governed Protestant church caused great problems for leading local families and their tenants who resolutely clung to the old faith. The early eighteenth-century diaries of Nicholas Blundell of Little Crosby portray a rural life of continuity with earlier centuries and integration between the various local settlements.

Much was to change in the following hundred years. New transport links were developed. The first commuters from Liverpool arrived, but this was as nothing compared with the building boom and population rises of the late nineteenth and early twentieth centuries. With them, the Crosby as we know it became a fact. Many of our local institutions which contribute so much to character of the place came into being. In the twenty-first century change continues.

ONE

The Shore and the Dunes

The shore is a good place to start because that is where the earliest evidence for human activity in the area has been found. This coast has always been and continues to be a dynamic environment. But back some 21,000 years ago the whole area was covered in a massive ice sheet. About 14,000 years ago this ice began to melt rapidly (in geological time) and retreat northwards. Four thousand years later the basin, which became the Irish Sea, had been flooded and the retreating ice had left behind the sand which covers much of the seabed and boulders which had been scooped up in its advance. Crosby has a famous example of one these 'erratic' boulders. This twenty-ton lump of gypsum probably came from the Lake District, and was excavated from the clay pit of the Crosby brick works in Cooks Lane in 1898. It was moved and placed on a plinth at the junction of Liverpool Road and Islington with iron railings round it. In 1926, it was moved to Coronation Park where it remains today.

As the ice retreated and the climate warmed, plants began to colonise the area. About 9,700 years ago birch trees were growing and some 2,500 years later they were joined by other species such as pine and oak. Evidence of this early afforestation was discovered on the shore and building excavations as fossilized tree stumps. There were also the remains of animals such as elk and deer. T. Mellarde Reade, the noted local architect, recorded these discoveries in the publications of the Liverpool Geological Society. Then the sea level rose again, flooding this landscape, and later left behind a large deposit of clay and the Downholland Silt which still underlies the sands.

There is no agreement about when the sand dunes, which were such a feature of this coast, began to form. One theory suggests that an offshore barrier allowed sand to accumulate about 6,000 years ago, and these dunes became part of the coast about 1,000 years later. Another suggests that some of the dunes were formed 6,000 years earlier. Dune building became faster from about 4,600 to 4,000 years ago as the sea level gradually dropped. Large amounts of dry sand were blown inland and deposited on top of existing peat bogs and this phenomenon can be seen at Hightown where the peat has been exposed below the dunes. Any shore is a dynamic environment and there were probably many more changes before the current set of dunes developed. The changes that happen to older dunes can be seen further up the coast where you can see a series of different environments reaching back from the present dunes. The strong winds, of which there are plenty, blowing in from the South West to the North West for most of the year shifted the dry dunes inland to form further dunes. This left patches of ground behind them, which went down to the level of the water table. These were known as slacks – marshy areas behind

The erratic boulder of gypsum found in the Cooks Road clay pit in 1898 and preserved as a relic in Coronation Park. Doubtless the local architect and geologist Thomas Mellarde Reade influenced the council to go to the expense of preserving this geological phenomenon.

Sand dunes and starr grass are still with us though large areas of dune have been covered in streets and houses. New dunes are forming all the time, such as those in front of the new swimming baths on Mariner's Road.

the beach dunes and the more consolidated formations inland. Plants, which could live on the minimum of nutrients, colonised the stable dunes and as they died and re-generated, organic matter built up. Different species began to take root to the point where the older dunes could grow small bushes of gorse and similar plants. The area, which is occupied with roads and buildings from Waterloo up to the coastguard station, was once an area of marsh and dunes. Indeed it was called Crosby Marsh and was an area set aside for the common grazing of sheep and cattle. It also contained a rabbit warren.

The dunes that are north of Blundellsands are believed to have been formed between AD 1200 and 1400, and may have continued forming up to the 1600s. In the eighteenth century local landowners assisted the consolidation of the dunes by planting marram grass (known as starr grass at that time). Tenants had a clause in their leases that obliged them to plant marram in the dunes and there was an Act of Parliament to ban the cutting of marram. Its tough flexible strands made it a useful material for thatching and making baskets and mats.

The shore has never remained entirely fixed. Blown sand often blocked drainage ditches. Moving dunes presented problems to the residents of Waterloo in the 1920s when its council had to set up a special Sand Removal Sub-Committee. Sefton MDC continues to manage the sand, which often threatens to submerge the beach promenade. Changes at the mouth of the River Alt resulted in severe erosion at Blundellsands in the first thirty years of the twentieth century, while record rainfall in December 1919 and January 1920 caused the Alt to alter its course even further inshore. The result was that fine seafront villas such as Netherwood, Beachside Towers, the Red House, Holmside, and later Edgewater lost their gardens and eventually succumbed themselves. The Alt was eventually diverted by building a training wall mainly of tin slag from a smelter in Litherland. During and after the Second World War large quantities of bricks and masonry was tipped on the shore as a sea defence north of Hall Road. This stretch of coast has seen increasing erosion in recent years with the cliff of rubble being eaten into year on year. So, nothing ever stays the same on the Crosby coastline.

No one knows when the first humans moved into the area. In 1929 a fine polished stone axe fashioned in the Lake District was found nearby. Unfortunately it was lost when Liverpool Museum was bombed in 1941. Many preserved footprints of man and various animals of the same era have been discovered on the shore at Formby and there was a small group of the same kind of prints found on the shore between Crosby coastguard station and Hightown in 2005 but, like the Formby prints, they were soon washed away.

The Celts, who began migrating to the Atlantic fringes of Europe from about the fifth century BC, found their way to the remote North West of England. The names Ince and Alt are Celtic and in 1978 a finely carved head possibly of a Celtic god was excavated from the garden of Strathearn in Crescent Road, Blundellsands. Two circular crop marks found by an aerial survey may be the sites of Romano-British farms. The only other local evidence for the Romans were two coins – one from the reign of the Emperor Nero of AD 64-66 and one of Claudius II, AD 268-70, found on the shore before 1939 and again lost in the destruction of Liverpool Museum.

This brings us up to the time when the Crosbys came into being. After the collapse of Roman government in the fifth century AD, England became fragmented between various kingdoms and peoples. The south and the east were gradually settled by the Angles, Saxons and the Jutes from Northern Germany, Denmark and Sweden. The native British peoples either co-existed with their new rulers or retreated to the west. The British kingdom of Rheged held the land between the Mersey and the Solway in the sixth century, and

A Celtic carved head found near the Leeds & Liverpool Canal at Lydiate. This is similar to one found at Crescent Road, Blundellsands, in 1978, for which a photograph cannot be found.

was conquered by Northumbria in the seventh century. But this was not the end of the upheavals of the Dark Ages. The Vikings, a warrior people mainly from Norway, began raids on the East Coast of England in the late ninth century which were followed by conquest of some of the Anglo-Saxon kingdoms. Later they settled around the West Coast of Scotland and the Irish Sea coastal fringes including the South West Lancashire and the Wirral. Scandinavian place names with a '-by' ending are common on both these coastlines. It is believed that this colonization was peaceful. On the other hand the discovery of a hoard of Anglo-Saxon coins at the Harkirk (another Scandinavian name) in Little Crosby in 1611 suggests that perhaps it was not as peaceful as all that.

These first Crosby settlers probably lived around what is now Great Crosby village. We do not know whether they arrived by sea or overland. The fact that they lived some way inland could suggest that they had turned their backs on the seagoing past. But the dunes stretched much further inland than they did in more recent times. It would have been unlikely that they did not carry on fishing because the local waters were noted for their fisheries. Fishing in the shallows could have been by means of hand nets or fish traps reaching out from the shore and it is possible that they had boats as well. There is not one piece of evidence for any of this. The River Alt was much wider then, and the tide went far inland possibly as far as Maghull. We do not know whether any boats sailed up, but a dug-out canoe was excavated right up at Huyton when they were building a railway there in the 1880s. There were certainly small ships, all of about twenty tons cargo capacity recorded as belonging to Altcar or Altmouth in the sixteenth and seventeenth centuries, and the remains of a stone quay were found near Grange Farm in the early 1900s. So there could have been maritime activity earlier on as well.

Boats that have used the River Alt: from small Viking cargo ships of the eleventh century to nineteenth-century fishing luggers, to the modern yachts of Blundellsands Sailing Club.

The smuggling of wines, tea and other foreign luxuries after 1671 from the Isle of Man was another activity along the shore. Nichols Blundell's Little Crosby diary recorded his share in this illegal business and the Collector of Customs at Liverpool admitted that the coast between Liverpool and Preston was very favourable for smuggling. His Riding Officers all lived about five or six miles apart and patrolled on their own. In 1750 he reported to London that smuggling was carried out from the Isle of Man 'in small boats that never appear on the coast but fall in with the land just in the dusk of the evening, that by their observations they may run in the night time into the place intended for the discharge of their goods where persons are always ready to assist and convey them to a proper place of safety.'

Fishing was also carried on. There is a fine oil painting in the Walker Art Gallery by Harry Williams dated 1856 which depicts the mouth of the Alt towards dusk with about half a dozen more two-masted fishing luggers. They would have been used for daily fishing trips into Liverpool Bay. Mannex's Directory of 1854 listed William Belton as a fisherman at Great Crosby and the 1888 Bootle and District Directory listed several fishermen living in Sawyer's Cottages in Crosby village. John 'Roast Beef' Jackson was a noted local character and fisherman at the turn of the twentieth century. He had built himself a shanty in the sand dunes in about 1871 and earned a living by fishing, cockling and beachcombing. Crosby in Camera has pictures of him outside his home and peddling his cockles from a creel basket. Today there is still the occasional fishing by tractors dragging a trawl net through the shallows.

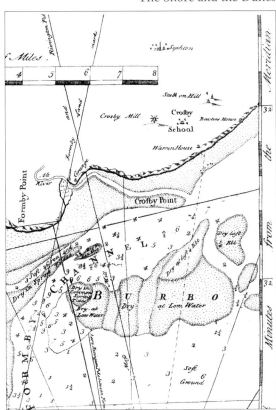

Fearon & Eye's chart of 1736 showing the entrance of the River Alt and Crosby Point. There were stone obelisk landmarks at Hightown which had to be lined up to make the right approach. Buildings such as the Warrener's house on Crosby Marsh, Crosby windmill and Sefton church are also marked as landmarks.

The Crosby shore is on the approaches to the Port of Liverpool. Given the complexity and unstable character of the offshore sand banks and the fierce gales blowing in from the North West it is not surprising that ships (especially sailing ships) were driven ashore here. The Lord of the Manor's right to claim any wreck cast upon the shore was mentioned as early as the fifteenth century. It must have been valuable because there was a dispute between the Crown who owned the manor and locals such as the Blundell family. They continued to claim the right to wrecked cargo down to the eighteenth century. In 1764, a smuggling vessel had been lost off the coast and thirty-two small barrels of rum came ashore which the Blundell's steward recovered. This was disputed by the Customs office in Liverpool, because under Common Law if a man or a dog escaped from the ship, it could not be considered a wreck. And what was more, the import of rum in small containers was prohibited.

If a ship did go ashore, it was a great temptation to the locals to plunder the cargo and the crew's possessions. There have been lots of legends about people deliberately setting up false lights to lure ships ashore, but recent research has shown that these were myths. Wrecking was opportunistic. I wonder how much local people got away with from the ship *Clarence*, which ran aground at Crosby in 1780. She had been inward-bound for Liverpool with a cargo from Jamaica. Although not specified, this cargo would no doubt have consisted of sugar and rum. The Customs spent a total of £112 13s 10d to salvage the cargo, which included £37 15s for labourers and £57 5s 10d for carting it away. Other expenses included ale, cheese and beef for the superintending Customs officers. As the

Above: Fishing by a tractor dragging a trawl net through the shallows is the last type of fishing apart from angling practised on the Crosby shore.

Left: The figurehead of the brigantine *Rosebud*, preserved for many years on the wall of Liverpool Building Materials store off Little Crosby Road in Crosby village.

labour, the carts, the ale, cheese and beef were probably supplied from Crosby, the locals profited legitimately as well.

Liverpool's increasing trade saw many more ships passing the Crosby shore. The port authorities took new measures to ensure the safe passage of ships. New charts of the Liverpool approaches were published and more seamarks, lighthouses and buoys and a compulsory pilotage service were all working by the 1780s. Fearon & Eye's chart of 1736 showed a sand bank jutting out from the Alt known as Crosby Point. It also showed landmarks ashore including Crosby windmill and the spire of Sefton church. Neither can be seen from the shore today because of the plantations of trees.

In the late 1830s Commander Denham RN found a new channel through the maze of Mersey sand banks. This new Victoria Channel (now Queen's Channel) ended off Hightown where it became the Crosby Channel. In 1840 this change was marked by a lightship and a lighthouse ashore. Later a second lighthouse was built because of the changing position of the channel. Today, both lighthouses have long gone, and the lightship was replaced in 1950 by a large red and white striped buoy. But the Crosby Channel is still the main approach and is stabilised by training banks of stone. Every tide sees huge container ships, ferries and tankers passing in and out of the port aided by a port radar system and their own navigational equipment including collision avoidance radar, echo depth sounders and global positioning systems. Nevertheless, all of them have to carry an experienced local pilot or a master who regularly makes the trip and has a pilotage exemption certificate.

Most of the shipping casualties of the later nineteenth and early twentieth centuries were either ships running ashore or through collisions in bad visibility. The Merseyside Maritime Museum has two relics of these notable strandings – a model of the Houston Line's steamer *Heraclides* and the figurehead from the sailing brigantine *Rosebud*. In October 1902, the *Heraclides* ran aground on Taylor's Bank. Her crew was rescued, and there was every indication that she was a total loss. However, she re-floated herself, drifted across the channel and ended up on Crosby beach. After a lot of digging and shifting 350 tons of coal bunkers, three tugs pulled her clear. The most likely ships to end up on Crosby beach were the small coasting schooners, which numbered hundreds. Many were employed in hauling china clay from Cornwall for delivery to Runcorn. In 1902, the brigantine *Rosebud* was wrecked at Formby, but somehow her figurehead was rescued and brought to Crosby. For many years, this wooden Victorian lady clutching her rose was mounted on a wall of a builder's yard in Crosby village. In the 1970s, the site was redeveloped and the figurehead was given to the museum. It was not in good condition and remains in store. The remains of the Henderson liner *Pegu*, which grounded on the Crosby Channel training bank in 1939, can still be seen off Hightown. Her foremast was a landmark until demolished by the tug *Wallasey* in 1987. Some of her export cargo of spirits found its way ashore, apparently to the delight of the residents of Hightown. Bottles would occasionally turn up from the *Pegu* as late as the 1970s, though the content tended to have a slightly salty tang. Strandings are rare occurrences today. The last major one was that of the Irish Sea ferry *European Leader*, which suffered an engine failure and drifted ashore off Hall Road in September 2000. She was quickly refloated without casualties or damage.

Another use of the shore was military. The complexity of the sand banks made an enemy sailing warship attack difficult. Nevertheless, Liverpool had gun batteries to drive off such raids from the eighteenth century. In the 1820s two substantial stone forts were built at New Brighton and Seaforth. The Seaforth battery disappeared with the building of Gladstone Dock, but its twin survives and is open to the public. It gives a good idea

A six-inch naval gun from the wreck of the White Star liner *Laurentic* torpedoed off Ireland in 1940 was the type of gun mounted at Fort Crosby. The propeller in the foreground comes from the 1964 tug *Brocklebank*, now preserved at the museum as a working vessel that passes Crosby several times a year on voyages to maritime festivals.

of what the Seaforth establishment must have been like. One of its thirty-two-pounder muzzle-loading cannon can be seen at the Maritime Museum. The local Artillery Volunteer Battery, started by Colonel Blundell in 1859, occupied Boundary Cottage, Little Crosby Road. They were equipped with another four thirty-two-pounders. Volunteer soldiers also made good use of the shore for annual camps where neat lines of bell tents were erected at Waterloo and in the establishment of a shooting range at Altcar in 1860. Fort Crosby was set up in the dunes north of the coastguard station in 1906. Most of it was demolished between 1964 and 1967, but the remains of brick bunkers can still be seen. It was armed with two six-inch naval guns and a similar one salvaged from the wreck of the White Star liner *Laurentic* is on the quay of the Maritime Museum. Other wartime installations included concrete tank traps and a Royal Observer Corps post at the bottom of Sandheys Avenue. In the First World War, there were also temporary army camps on what were then fields of Moor Lane. The other development of the shore was the establishment of a seaside resort at Waterloo, but that story has to wait until chapter three.

TWO

Rural Crosby

Crosby today is an urban area with some open spaces such as parks in its centre and with farming on the periphery of 'Greater Crosby', which takes in Little Crosby and Thornton.

Even 100 years ago, there were farms and cow keepers' establishments within its own boundaries. And 100 years before then, agriculture was the predominant activity. In 1811, the second population census for the United Kingdom showed that forty-five per cent of the local population was engaged in agriculture. But as the canal, the roads and the railway opened the area for well-to-do people to build houses and for day trips from Liverpool, so the numbers of farm workers declined. By the 1861 census, the percentage had more than halved to just over twenty per cent and twenty years later, in 1881, it had halved again to ten per cent. I am indebted to Roger Hull's MA thesis: 'Social differentiation in a north Liverpool suburb: the case of Great Crosby and Waterloo, 1841-1901' for these figures. If you want to gain a more detailed picture of population and social changes in nineteenth-century Crosby, then you can find a copy in the Local History Library at Waterloo.

The evidence for the first farmsteads comes from aerial surveys carried out by the Liverpool Museum in the 1980s and 1990s. A circular Romano-British enclosure was spotted in the fields to north of Little Crosby Hall and another possible site was identified near Oaklands Cottage on the southern edge of the hall's park, one field away from Little Crosby Road.

At the time of the Domesday survey, it was one of six settlements in the Hundred of West Derby. A hundred was an administrative unit of land, which notionally supported a hundred families and went back to Anglo-Saxon times before the Norman Conquest of England in 1066. It was also the administrative unit for gathering the king's taxes and for trying minor law suits. It was owned by the royal family and in about 1189 Richard I gave it to his brother John – 'Bad Prince John' of the Robin Hood legends – who ruled England while his brother was away crusading in the Holy Land. John in turn rented it out to his servant Robert De Ainsdale for an annual rent of 100 shillings. The De Ainsdales adopted the name Blundell in the thirteenth century.

From 1211 the manor of Little Crosby was held by the Molyneux family who were also constables of the royal castle at Liverpool and hence a real power locally. In 1327, it was granted to a younger son, Roger De Molyneux, who in turn passed it on to his son Roger. This younger Roger had no children and so the manor was left to his sister Agnes who married David Blundell of Great Crosby about 1362. Their descendants continue to live at Little Crosby Hall – one of the few landed families left in Lancashire. Great Crosby

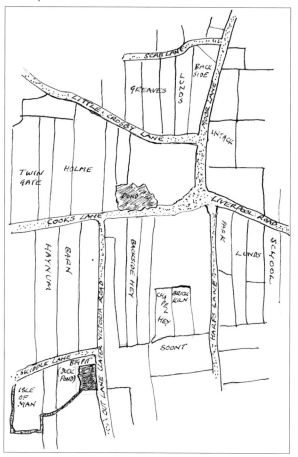

Great Crosby village and its surrounding fields taken from the Tithe Map of 1844.

remained in royal hands until 1625. Charles I, who was always short of money and never keen to try to extract more from his fractious parliaments, sold it to the Molyneux family for £12,000. In 1798, they sold it to the Blundells.

Like many other Lancashire villages, Great Crosby had a mixed economy of arable land and animals. The arable fields were laid out in the open field system. Apparently, it was not the classic three-field system, which you read about in history textbooks, but one large town field. Long narrow strips or butts were allocated to individual peasant farmers. Aerial photographs taken in the 1980s suggest that some of the strips survive from the Thornton fields just to the north of the crematorium. They were leased or rented from the lord of the manor and the rent was mainly paid in kind. The kind part was a number of hens to be handed to the lord at Easter and boon work, which was a fixed number of days of work on the lord's own demesne land. According to Charles Lamb's history of Crosby, the standard annual rent for five acres was four shillings and sixpence in the Middle Ages. There was also a much larger cash payment (a fine) paid when a new person took over the tenancy. In addition there was also a tax in kind or tithe or tenth of produce due to the Church. Tithes were often stored in a barn owned by the Church. This barn is commemorated by the naming of the little group of houses off Moor Lane near the windmill known as 'The Tithebarn'.

The grazing land was mainly a communal facility. Tenants were allowed a fixed number of animals on the commons to avoid over-grazing. At Great Crosby the common areas were on the periphery of the village. To the north and east of the village there were commons called the Moor and Brownmoor. These names are perpetuated in Moor Lane and some of the roads leading off it and in Brownmoor Lane. The biggest common was Crosby Marsh, which was behind the swathe of sand dunes which stretched right along the coast to Hightown. The marsh had other uses. It provided peat as a source of fuel and part of it was a rabbit warren with a house for the warrener. Rabbits were valuable for their meat and their fur. The warren was still going in the early nineteenth century and its location still commemorated by Warrenhouse Road. It is noticeable that this has an irregular route unlike all the later straight roads on either side of it. The first detailed Ordnance Survey map of the area, published in 1850, also shows a second warren house on Sandy Lane, Hightown.

Arable farming techniques gradually changed over the centuries. At first, it was very much a subsistence economy where each family provided for itself with possibly a surplus at harvest time, which could be sold to buy goods they could not produce themselves. Yields were low compared with more recent times. Sections of the field would be left fallow and used for grazing on a rotating pattern. This allowed the land to recover and to be manured by the dung of the grazing beasts. Apart from animal manure the only fertilizers available

Marl or brick pit? The large pond at Park House on the corner of Haigh Road and Crosby Road North, Waterloo, was hidden from view (unless you were on a double-decker bus) until its wall was taken down for rebuilding in the autumn of 2005.

Part of the huge collection of farm implements in the Village Museum, including a large wooden grain or malt shovel to the right of centre.

T. Silcock's horse-drawn lorry built in Liverpool about 1920 was used to deliver produce from Edge Farm on the Sefton-Thornton boundary to market in Liverpool.

Brown Moor lay outside the main field and the fields of Brownmoor Farm may have been taken out of the Moor in about 1602. The existing farmhouse is believed to date from about 1830.

were lime, ashes from the burned moss of undrained land, seaweed and marl. Marl, was a mixture of clay, lime and sand, was dug out from pits and spread on the land about every twenty years. It was supposed to renew the fertility of the soil. Marling was extensively practiced on the Crosby fields and the evidence for this is in the numerous pits that are marked on the 1907 Ordnance Survey map. You can see this in the original maps held at the Local History Library or in the reprint, which Alan Godfrey Maps have published recently. You can also find isolated ponds in the fields to the north of Thornton, which must have been marl pits, and the large pond at Park House, Waterloo, might have been a marl pit or possibly a clay pit although there is no record of brick making there. More powerful fertilizers, which were usually rich in nitrates and phosphates, did not become available until the mid-nineteenth century. Two that could have been used early on in Crosby were guano and bonemeal. Guano was seabird droppings, which had accumulated in huge deposits on the islands off the coast of Peru. It was first imported to Liverpool in 1840. Bonemeal was made from cattle bones crushed by new steam-powered machinery and treated with sulphuric acid to make 'superphosphate'. Preparing the seed bed by ploughing and harrowing (to break up the larger lumps of soil) was all done with horses and sowing was done by 'broadcasting', that is scattering seed by hand from a basket slung round the sower's waist. In the nineteenth century horse-drawn seed drills were invented, which sowed the seed more economically in rows. There are some good examples of horse-drawn ploughs and other farm implements in the Little Crosby Village Museum.

One of the major drawbacks of the old way of farming was that not enough winter feed could be grown for the farm animals. As a result most of the sheep and cattle, apart from the breeding stock, were slaughtered before the onset of winter and their meat salted down. The introduction of root crops such as turnips, swedes and mangel-wurzels in the middle of the eighteenth century provided the answer. These needed to be chopped up before the animals could consume them. At first this was done with a special hand implement. By the late nineteenth century there were powered root crop cutters available. There are several of these on display in Little Crosby Village Museum and also two used as garden ornaments.

The arrangements for the land changed over time. The open field was supplemented by fenced fields and meadows usually known as crofts and heys. New arable land was added by reclaiming some of the grazing land. The large section of Brownmoor on the Rimrose Valley was put under the plough at some point possibly in the early seventeenth century. There is a record of 200 acres being enclosed in 1602. You can see this in the shape of the field boundaries alongside Brownmoor Farm on the 1907 Ordnance Survey map. It is also noticeable that field number 256, next to the footpath leading to the Leeds & Liverpool Canal, is a strip or butt in its original common field form. This was a very unusual survival because from the sixteenth century onwards the land was gradually parcelled up into separate fields. The biggest change was probably the enclosure of the main common grazing area – Crosby Marsh – in 1816. The layout of the fields just before the first urban expansion can be seen well on the Tithe Award map of 1844. This was drawn up as a result of the Tithe Commutation Act of 1836 which commuted all tithe payments in kind to a cash payment. There is a modern version drawn from the original in the Lancashire Record Office in the Crosby Local History Library. This is a truly fascinating document. The first thing to strike you is the variety of field names. There are the obvious ones such as the heys such as Toad, Williamson's or Barn and the crofts such as Mullineux, Orchard or Barn. Then there are the descriptive ones such as Brick Kiln or Broken Field, and the obscure such as Sniddle, Brunchards, Cow Wham and Cubber's Acre. There are also the humorous such as Lousy Croft and Isle of Man, which was a field which was surrounded on three sides by a stream that ran from the present-day Duck Pond in Victoria Road to the north. A few field names have survived in the names of roads, and these include Forefield, Brownmoor, Merrilocks, Oaklands, Stanfield as in Stanfield House and Handfield in Waterloo. Endbutt is another, but it appears to have been changed from Henbutts. It has been suggested that this was an area for poultry rearing. Apart from the field of that name that lay between Liverpool Road and Endbutt Road, the Hall Mote records for 7 January 1856 mentioned a tenancy known as the Henbutts (a farmhouse, two cottages and four outbuildings) which was 'bounded to the north and the east by Henbutts Lane'. So, this might have been the chicken farm This goes against the commonly held belief that Endbutt was derived from 'End Boat' because it was the road you took to catch the packet boat on the Leeds & Liverpool Canal.

Most farms were more like peasant's smallholdings than farms as we understand them today. Even as late as 1844, seventy-five per cent of the land holdings were under five acres. However, the soil was and still is of the highest quality. It is not clear when these smallholdings were merged to form larger units but even today many farms in the district are quite small at about the fifty-acre mark. The biggest landowners were William Blundell with 1,300 acres and Henry Myers, who gave his name to Myers Road, with 181 acres. Improvements to the land, the introduction of new crops and the improved breeding of animals were usually the work of the landlords who had the education, the time and the money. Nicholas Blundell, whose diary gives us so much insight into life in Crosby in

Jump's Carrfield Dairy was housed in this late nineteenth-century building. The gables on the left of the building were loading doors for fodder for the cows.

the early eighteenth century, tried new crops such as maize and imported cattle from other parts of the country. He also bought and studied books on agriculture.

The landlord governed the village and its land through the Hall Mote or manor court. The records of the Hall Motes of local manors including Great Crosby have been transcribed by the late Thomas Williams of Thornton – a real labour of love. There are copies in the Crosby Local History Library. Systematic records started to be kept from the thirteenth century. In Crosby's case, they start in 1452 and run right up to 1884. The Mote was expected to ensure that the lord's rights, such as the fines on new tenants, were protected, to enforce local bylaws and to check the quality of locally made bread and ale – life's two essentials. There were a number of elected posts including two constables, two ale tasters and two bylaw men and a jury of four reeves to try any disputed matters. For example, on 21 June 1463 Henry Nicholson was fined three pence for not paying his half of the rent of a 'fish stall'. Allocation of fishing on the beach was partitioned into 'stalls' and an annual rent was payable to the lord of the manor. The rabbit warren was also reserved to the lord and in January 1539 Henry Lathwayt of Ormskirk, Henry Ambrose and Richard Hatton were fined two shillings for running a greyhound in the rabbit warren. Most of the entries were concerned with the upkeep of the land itself. Blown sand was a continuing problem because it clogged the drainage ditches. In November 1515 all the tenants were ordered to scour their ditches by the time of the Feast of the Annunciation (25 March) on pain of a three shillings and fourpence fine. It also fined tenants for overstocking the common grazing areas or for dumping rubbish. Stray animals were caught and confined to the pound or pinfold near the centre of the village until the owner came forward to claim them and pay a fine. The pinfold is recalled in the name of the flats Pinfold Court at the junction of Alexandra Road and Islington. The elected officers were increased in the sixteenth and seventeenth centuries to include overseers of the poor and starr grass lookers. Later records tended to be concerned with the entry of new tenants as the Mote's jurisdiction was superseded by other local courts.

As the urban population of England grew larger and larger in the eighteenth and nineteenth centuries, farms with access to roads or canals could prosper by supplying fresh fruit, vegetables, milk, meat and eggs to shopkeepers and wholesale markets in the towns. In exchange, the town supplied the farms with large quantities of horse manure and what was politely termed 'night soil' for fertilizing the fields. The demand for fresh produce encouraged the growing of potatoes. Nicholas Blundell had only grown them as a garden crop for his own consumption, but they became one of the main crops from the end of the eighteenth century. The Village Museum has some examples of the special ridging ploughs which were used to heap up earth around the potato tubers. As the road to Liverpool was improved, it was possible for farmers to carry their own produce into Liverpool. Four-wheel flat wagons were introduced in the mid-nineteenth century to replace the traditional two-wheel cart in order to increase carrying capacity. These market garden 'lorries' were light enough to be pulled by one horse. There is a fine example of one in the National Museums Liverpool's transport collection. This was owned by Silcocks who farmed at Edge Farm which was just across the border in Sefton. Unfortunately it has been taken off display and is in store and can only be seen by appointment.

J. Dugdale,

Cowkeeper & Farmer

CROSBY . . . . .
MODERN DAIRY,

Carnegie Avenue (Coronation Road),
Opposite New Library, GREAT CROSBY.

Families supplied at their own residences with Genuine New Milk and Cream twice daily. Special Cows kept for Infants and Invalids.

FRESH BUTTER AND NEW LAID EGGS EVERY MORNING.
- - Inspection Invited. - -

A 1909 advertisement for Dugdale's Dairy, Carnegie Road.

Orchard Farm, off Alexandra Road, is notable for having one side of its roof still covered with its original stone flags.

Apart from the road names, there are few surviving fragments of Crosby's rural past. Perhaps the best known is the Duck Pond in Victoria Road. This was a farm pond for Wright's Big Pit Farm. In its later years, having lost its fields to house building, it was a dairy with milk supplied from Little Crosby. The farm buildings were demolished to make way for flats in the 1960s. Brownmoor Farm house survives and is believed to date to about 1830 and the barn behind it which has been converted into a house may date back to the eighteenth century. Ivy Farm, a house probably dating from the late nineteenth century, is at the Brownmoor Lane end of Endbutt Lane. Jump's Carrfield Model Dairy survives as the Simply Food and Drinks shop at the junction of Myers Road East and Stuart Road. Jump's grazed their cows on the remains of the Crosby Marsh pastures in front of the Esplanade at Waterloo before the building of the gardens in 1931 There is a good photograph in the revised edition of J. Lewis's *The Birth of Waterloo*. J. Dugdale, 'cowkeeper and farmer', had his modern dairy at Carnegie Avenue opposite the library. According to his 1913 advertisement, 'Families supplied at their own residences with Genuine New Milk and Cream twice daily. Special cows kept for infants and invalids.' Adulteration and watering down was common in the Good Old Days. The little café building and Nixon and Gallegher's building behind it were probably part of this establishment. The Blundell's Chase homes on College Road North have been converted from another similar dairy. Cowkeeping was a local practice around Liverpool where the cows were fed indoors for most of the year. But to see what farm buildings were like before Crosby became a suburb, you have to go to Little Crosby, Thornton or Sefton. Little Crosby has the added asset of its museum and its knowledgeable curator Bob Wright. Its collections include a vast number of agricultural tools and equipment, which were all used in and around Crosby in the nineteenth and twentieth centuries.

THREE
Villas, Semis and Terraces

In the nineteenth century the fields and farmsteads of Crosby retreated as the number of houses increased. In 1800, there was a village centre at the junction of Liverpool Road, Moor Lane and Little Crosby Road with a green and St Michael's chapel. There were also isolated farms and cottages. Development began next to the seashore. The enclosure and parcelling up of Crosby Marsh opened up the possibility of developing a sea bathing resort. Bathing in the sea became a fashionable alternative to attending inland spas from the middle of the eighteenth century. Sea water was considered to have all kinds of health-giving properties. The early resorts, especially Brighton, were patronised by royalty and high society, and the quest for health was linked with all sorts of other amusements such as boating trips, concerts and dancing. The sea bathing fashion called for the building of hotels, lodging houses and shops. It was also taken up by the wealthier middle classes, and resort towns such as Southport and Blackpool grew rapidly from about 1800. In the North West, there was a tradition of sea bathing in August when 'the physick of the sea' was believed to be strongest. This attracted not just the respectable and bathing naked was usual. Ellen Weeton, who was lodging at Beacon's Gutter, the Bootle resort, recorded in her diary for 7 August 1809: 'I am sat writing in a bedroom window that overlooks the river, and often raise my head to look at the vessels, and see the people bathing – the latter is not the most delicate sight, but I am now so accustomed to it, that I do not feel so shocked as I ought to do'.

The Mersey had other smaller bathing resorts apart from Beacon's Gutter, which included places as far upriver as Runcorn. By 1816 sea bathing was going on at Crosby Seabank, where the first hotel, the Royal Waterloo, was opened that year. The obscure Belgian village of Waterloo had become famous the previous year as the place where Napoleon had been finally defeated by Wellington. Bathing was not without controversy because both the local landowners, Blundells and Molyneux, questioned the right of the hotel proprietors to operate bathing machines on the beach. Within ten years, Waterloo had grown to include the start of Marine Crescent, East Street and South Street (later South Road). There were two lodging houses, a post office and grocery and other essential suppliers such as a wine merchant and a confectioner. Marine Crescent and subsequent additions were constructed as terraces. They followed the style of Georgian seaside architecture in other resorts. Their brickwork smoothed over with stucco in imitation of stone and painted, and they were provided with delicate cast-iron and glass verandas overlooking the shore.

The houses behind these terraces in East Street, Duke Street etc. were much smaller and rented out as shops and accommodation for servants and tradesmen. To the north, a second

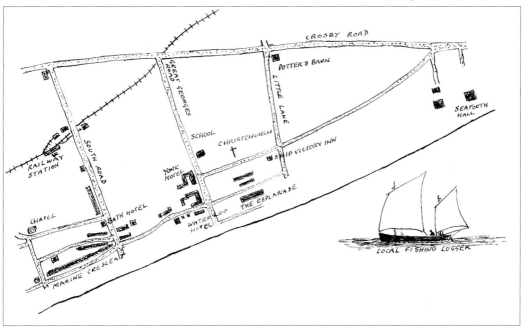

Waterloo streets in 1850.

smaller resort, which was ambitiously named Brighton Le Sands, was started in 1822-23 with two sets of terraced houses in Mersey View. It never caught on, unlike New Brighton across the Mersey, which had the advantage of a steam ferry service to Liverpool from 1833.

The village of Great Crosby remained a separate rural entity rather like the present-day village of Little Crosby although the latter's houses are much more spacious and better built. The majority of the dwellings were small, thatched cottages. This was the traditional form along the whole of this part of the coast. Many were single-storey, partly because of poverty and partly to present a low profile to the constant winds. There are other examples of this humble type of dwelling in Formby and Churchtown. These are now highly valued examples of architectural heritage and desirable as properties because they are so different to the mass of modern housing around them. At the time of their construction they were the homes of reasonably well-off yeomen – small landholding farmers. The dwellings of the poor labourers were much smaller and primitive, and have entirely disappeared.

It is difficult to imagine just how isolated the parish was before 1850. John Kidde who was appointed headmaster of Merchant Taylors' School in 1643, told his patrons, the company of Merchant Taylors in London, that 'The situation of the school is in the most desolate and obscure angle of the county... Besides popery, the extreme poverty, I will not say beggary of the country is no small rub'.

Little Crosby Hall was and is the premier house. First constructed in 1609, possibly on the site of an earlier house, it survives though greatly changed, in the ownership of the descendants of the original family. One step down, there were some substantial houses mainly along Liverpool Road dating from the early nineteenth century. They were large detached dwellings built in a variety of styles. Belle Vue (117 Liverpool Road) is probably

Left: Belle Vue, 117 Liverpool Road, is one of several examples of early nineteenth-century houses along Liverpool Road. The buildings to the left and right appear to be extensions.

Below: 37 Victoria Road, a nicely restored example of a smaller Georgian house. It features on the left-hand side of the Armstrong's 1881 advertisement because their premises were next door.

Harrocks House, Victoria Road, Great Crosby looks as if it was built in the mid-nineteenth century. It has a stuccoed ground floor with a bay and a nice round arched entrance. The older (heavily restored) eighteenth-century cottage next to it may be the original Harrocks House.

one of the oldest – a plain Georgian house with a ground floor raised over a basement and steps to an entrance with fluted Doric pillars, and a covering of stucco which has later been pebble-dashed except for the quoins at its corners. The Georgian style was based on the re-interpretation of Greek and Roman architecture by the seventeenth-century Italian architect Palladio. It emphasised simplicity, symmetry, form and proportion and was widely used not only in the great stately houses, but for town houses and terraces. Crosby House, which is part of Nazareth House is another substantial Georgian house. Number 37 Victoria Road is a good example of a smaller Georgian house with its large sash windows and semicircular fanlight over its front door. There are several similar examples, which are either terraces or semi-detached on either side of the Moor Lane roundabout. There is another terrace next to St Peter and St Paul's church with a raised ground floor and 155 has a rainwater head dated 1826.

On Victoria Road, Great Crosby, there is the much-altered terrace – Springfield Cottages – which is the last surviving workers' terrace in Great Crosby built before 1850. Harrocks House in the same road was mentioned in the Great Crosby Hallmote (village court) records in 1760 as 'the site of a cottage lately called Harrocks House'. The present house is of a later date of a later style with the ground floor stuccoed in imitation of bands of stonework, a nice round arch for the entrance with moulded decoration and a tall gable with bay windows. Number 44 Victoria Road, next door, is a late eighteenth-century (much restored) detached house, and may be the rebuilt Harrocks House referred to in the records.

Above left: Coyne Learmouth's offices, 135 Liverpool Road, is a semi-detached house probably of the 1860s with Italianate features such as the moulded cornice and string courses and nicely carved keystone over the ground-floor window.

Above right: Ellesmere House, Crosby Road North, is another large villa with Italianate features such as the extravagantly leafy capitals and the stuccoed spandrels imitating stonework. The bust on the keystone appears to be carved from life – perhaps the daughter of the first owner.

The Italianate style became increasingly fashionable from the late 1840s, and the well-off favoured it because it allowed a more individual appearance for their homes than the Georgian style. This was inspired by features of Italian Renaissance palaces and was taken up by Victoria and Albert for their seaside home Osborne House (1849) on the Isle of Wight. Shallow-pitched overhanging roofs with decorative cornices or brackets, porches with columns and horizontal string courses were some of the features passed down to middle-class villas. Ellesmere House on Crosby Road North, Waterloo, and Coyne Learmouth, the solicitor's office, 135 Liverpool Road, are two good examples among many local villas with a touch of the Italianate. Perhaps the best is Winchester House, Beach Lawn, which was built for Thomas Ismay in 1865. The decorative cornice modelled in moulded bricks remained popular for later local houses.

The Gothic architecture of the Middle Ages was introduced for new churches and houses from about the 1820s, and most of the local churches and great institutions such as Merchant Taylors' School (1878) were built in this fashion. Thanks to the works of John Ruskin such as *The Seven Lamps of Architecture* of 1849 and the subsequent publication of builder's pattern books, it came to be a major influence in suburban architecture. This new Gothic was greatly simplified and featured asymmetric frontages with bay windows, steep roofs, pointed arches,

Streatham House, 1874 – a good example of a Gothic villa, with tall narrow proportions and pointed window brickwork in multi-coloured brick.

carved capitals to the windows and doors and different coloured brick patterns on their walls. The two seaside terraces of Brighton Le Sands are the first houses to have Gothic features. Stanfield House on Liverpool Road, which was also built before 1850, has tall Gothic proportions and a Perpendicular entrance door lintel with traceried fanlight. Similar Gothic elements can be found on 57 Moor Lane with its fine carved tracery gateposts.

Waterloo and Great Crosby grew separately. In 1856, Waterloo-with-Seaforth formed a separate local Board of Health. Great Crosby was placed under a separate body in 1863. The Urban District Councils that replaced them did not merge until 1936. As late as 1888 a local directory described Great Crosby as 'an old-fashioned straggling village'. The 1851 railway link to Liverpool appears to have benefited both, though Waterloo station was right in the middle of the resort while the other's was at a distance from the village itself. The railway enabled far more middle-class professional people to move out of the polluted heart of Liverpool and travel to work from there.

The expansion of the middle classes was a national phenomenon in Victorian Britain. Their homes, which were often rented rather than purchased, had to reflect their status and their respectability. The house designs tended to emphasise the frontages. So, for example, it might be built of better-quality brick with decorative features and have a clear demarcation of the front boundary with brick walls often topped with iron railings. It also saw the laying out of streets in a grid pattern filling in the fields between Crosby Road and the older waterfront houses. For example, St John's Road was planned in the 1860s and a series of streets of terraced houses were eventually built off it including Argo, Corona, Lyra and Norma to the south. These were clearly one development, which probably dates from the 1870s. You can see how other groups of streets were developed en bloc from the shared theme of their names. For example, on the opposite side of St John's Road there is a group of streets which all end in 'dale'.

A dated example of the vernacular pebble-dashed style of semi-detached houses, designed by the younger Mellard Reade for the Blundells in 1910. The original elevation drawing is in the Village Museum, Little Crosby.

People who took these houses were 'respectable' families. Many of the breadwinners were associated with sea and included master mariners, marine engineers and customs officers. The Victorians stressed the importance of the home and the family, and the home in the suburbs was separated from work. Living over the shop became less common and more socialising was done at home. This in turn saw a change in the internal lay-out of houses. In the eighteenth century, rooms had many uses and servants ate and slept in areas shared with their masters. The Victorian era saw the development of segregated rooms with a specific purpose. There was the 'best room' or drawing room which was richly furnished and reserved for formal entertaining and Sundays, a dining room, a morning room or parlour for day-to-day use, a separate kitchen and scullery and separate bedrooms upstairs. The more advanced houses might have a bathroom and a water closet. This lay-out was repeated at various sizes in middle-class terraces, semi-detached and detached houses.

The emphasis on the family was also reflected in the way local shops advertised themselves as 'family' butchers, grocers or dairymen. Respectability was also associated with attending church and as the houses were built, so the number, size and different denominations of local places of worship increased.

Great Crosby and Waterloo were also attractive to the wealthy. In 1865 Nicholas Blundell instructed the Liverpool firm of Mellard Reade & Goodison to draw up a plan for developing the dunes to the north of Brighton Le Sands as 'a residential place for the better classes'. The development was set around a twenty-acre Key Park which still preserves some of the old dunes. It was laid out with wide streets and large plots (quarter of an acre upwards). The central feature was the curving Serpentine. The same firm produced a later design for Hightown, which consisted of two heart-shaped avenues crossed by an intersecting straight road. This was never built because it was considered to be too close to the Alt, which was beginning to erode the beach. This grand plan is on display at the Village Museum. Development at Blundellsands was slow at first. A mock-Tudor house next to the railway station dated 1866 and the grand terrace on Warren Road designed by Mellarde Reade for the Blundells, dated 1867, were probably the first two houses. Progress was quicker from the 1880s when wealthy shipowners such as Sir William Forwood and Thomas Goffey had 'Ramleh' and 'Amalfi' built on Burbo Bank Road.

Waterloo Park was a similar though smaller development also intended for the really well-off. It seems to have been planned around 1870. There were also a number of very large detached and semi-detached houses lining Crosby Road South in Seaforth, Crosby Road North in Waterloo and in the streets between Cambridge Road and Great Georges Road. Quite a few have now been demolished, and others have been turned into flats or offices. The most southerly, 'Riverslie', with its cast-iron veranda, is now a nursing home, while 'Colonsay' at the junction with Cambridge Road belongs to the Mersey Mission to Seafarers.

The years from the late 1880s up to the outbreak of the First World War in 1914 were a boom time for all types of house building in the district. In 1888, Waterloo had twenty builders, while Great Crosby had eight and three masons. There was a change in appearance of the new houses. Up to the 1880s most houses were built of mainly local materials apart from their slate roofs. In that decade millions of bricks from Accrington or Ruabon in North Wales were brought in to build yet more new terraces.

Also from about the 1880s a new style inspired by English vernacular architecture, particularly the farms and cottages of South East England, began to take root. As the old way of country life declined, so its romantic attractiveness grew – forgetting all about the rural slums and the dire poverty of most country dwellers. Books on old country crafts, oak furniture and old cottages and magazines such as *Country Life* all fostered this nostalgia. William Morris and the Arts and Crafts Movement, and architects such as Norman Shaw and Alfred Voysey, were all highly influential in fashioning the new forms. It was translated into suburban architecture to give a different appearance to the new estates of houses. The availability of books of plans meant that the style could be readily copied. Many dwellings were given front gables, bay or oriel windows, mock-Tudor half timbering and leaded lights. Rough cast 'pebble-dash' wall finishes, clay tiles instead of slate, tiles hung on walls, ornamental plasterwork, moulded brick ornament, wrought-iron gates were some of the other ingredients to give a cottage veneer, a cosy feel to these otherwise mass-produced semi-detached suburban home. In the more exclusive suburbs, such as Blundellsands, there were individually designed houses, which echoed the same nostalgic forms.

The start of the twentieth century saw the re-introduction of Classical designs as interpreted by seventeenth-century architects alongside all the English vernacular bits. It was often seen in public buildings as 'Edwardian Baroque' and can be seen locally in the former Waterloo Grammar School, the NatWest Bank, Crosby Road North and the Seaforth Arms, Seaforth. 'Redcot', Warren Road of 1913, which is built in a late seventeenth-century English ('William and Mary') style is the best local domestic example. In more diluted form, many corner houses in the district have been decorated with circular or oblong turrets in the manner of French chateaux.

Turrets became a popular feature for corner site houses around 1900, This is wedge-shaped example at the corner of Coronation Road and York Avenue is clad in the popular small flat tiles. Note the rows of tile with curved bottoms to give variety.

The naming and layout of streets also changed. Avenues and Drives became popular in place of the more prosaic Streets or Roads and many were sinuous and not straight and wide enough to accommodate trees. The rural motifs, though watered down, still appeared in homes built after the First World War. It was also reflected in the names of new roads such as Rosedale Avenue, Rosemoor Drive, Greenway or Oaklands Avenue. Building houses was virtually unregulated until the late nineteenth century. The result too often, especially in large towns, was thousands of gerry-built houses with damp rooms and minimal sanitation. On the whole this did not apply to our district. Local authorities were given new powers, starting with the Public Health Act of 1875, to demolish slum properties, regulate the minimum size of rooms, ceiling heights, the gaps between the houses, provide sewerage and clean water and other measures to promote health. Certainly some of the smaller terrace houses such as Sawyer's Cottages rented by labourers and fishermen off Islington were very cramped and were eventually demolished.

In 1909, local councils were also made responsible to plan land use. Most of the open land in Waterloo had been built over, and more new houses were built when other users such as the football and cricket clubs moved from Waterloo Park. This re-use of scarce land for houses and flats has continued. A recent example is the replacement of Waterloo High School for Girls (later an annexe of Chesterfield High School) with houses. The same

There is a great variety of semi-detached house designs within the basic form. Quite often neighbouring houses were given different frontages. These photographs were all taken in a small area off Liverpool Road. From left to right, top to bottom: :Warwick Road hipped roof with bay windows and a porch; Coronation Drive slate hipped roof, large stone lintels and oriel window over the front door; Coronation Drive pebble-dashed with front gables and bays, semi-circular entrance; Liverpool Road with mansard roof, pebble-dashed top floor, curved bays, oriel windows; Liverpool Road with swept gables which were a feature designed by Alfred Voysey, pebble-dashed with simple half timbering and heavy stone lintels; Liverpool Road 1930s design with Westmorland slate hipped roof of a different profile and steel-framed windows at the corners of the buildings.

TELE^{PHONE}_{GRAMS} 1358 WATERLOO.

O. E. ROBERTS
Builder

40, KINGSWAY,
WATERLOO.

Left: O.E. Roberts' advertisement from 1929 featured a superior house detached and pebble-dashed of the kind built in Blundellsands.

Below: The English baroque style of the late seventeenth and early eighteenth century known as 'Queen Anne' was authentically copied at Redcot, Blundellsands by F. Atkinson in 1913. Other variations can be seen in the old Waterloo Grammar School, Cambridge Road, and the Seaforth Arms, Seaforth.

Above left: There are relatively few local Modernist houses. Banleen in St Michael's Road, Blundellsands, is one example of this uncompromising style with the frontage split between two well-proportioned blocks. Note also the steel-framed windows with a horizontal emphasis and no visible roof.

Above right: Alexandra Court, 2004, is one of several new developments that have returned to Victorian and Edwardian forms and materials including a Flemish gable, a corner turret and slate roof with an enigmatic cast-iron goddess of Alexandra Park in the foreground.

process has been at work in Blundellsands where large houses with gardens up to an acre have been demolished to make way for blocks of low-rise flats.

In the 1920s, the suburban expansion continued probably faster than before mainly on the north side of Crosby and over the parish boundary into Thornton. They were often much smaller than earlier homes, and were designed to be run by the housewife without the help of servants. The demand was supported by the increasing availability of mortgages from building societies. In the early 1930s, new houses, which were mainly semi-detached, could be bought from about £800 upwards. In 1933, John Alexander offered three- or four-bedroom houses on the Kenilworth estate (all the names were inspired by the titles of novels by Sir Walter Scott) from £885 to £1,350. In the same year, O.E. Roberts was offering houses in Esplen Avenue for £1,100 including a garage – another new feature – and an outside wash-house.

Another new aspect of housing development was the power given to local councils to build houses for renting to those who could not afford to buy. Early examples include the houses erected by Sefton Rural District in Edge Lane and Runnells Lane in the 1920s. The expansion northwards was checked by laws such as the 1935 Ribbon Development Act and the 1948 Town and Country Planning Act. The latter introduced the Green Belt around urban areas.

Crosby Curiosities

The Second World War placed Crosby directly in the front line along with the rest of Bootle and Liverpool. The port was essential to the British war effort and the German bombing campaign reached a peak in May 1941. In all over 9,000 houses were damaged and 415 were destroyed. The remaining fields in Thornton up to Lydiate Lane and off Little Crosby Road saw further building including council houses and old people's bungalows. Perhaps the biggest change in the local housing landscape since the Second World War was the building of tower blocks in the centre of Waterloo and on the site of Seaforth Barracks. Today home building continues on sites won from demolishing older buildings. For example, at the time of writing, the derelict Victorian Alexandra Hall has been replaced by Alexandra Court's 'exclusive apartments'. It is interesting to note that this and many other recent houses in the locality have returned to Victorian materials and designs with slate roofs and decorative brick work.

FOUR
Transport and Commerce

Great Crosby and especially Waterloo were able to expand in the nineteenth century because their links with Liverpool were radically improved. At first there was no direct road to Liverpool. Nicholas Blundell, the eighteenth-century diarist, and his contemporaries often preferred to ride along the shore to and from Liverpool. There was a through road by 1830 because about that year Samuel Towers of the Waterloo Hotel started a horse bus service to the Angel Inn, Liverpool, and in 1837 the service was extended to Crosby, and by 1848 there were twenty-eight round trips every day.

The opening of the Lancashire section of the Leeds & Liverpool Canal in 1774 was another improvement, and our district benefited because coal could be supplied cheaply from Wigan. There was also a regular passenger barge to Liverpool, and local farmers were able to move their produce into Liverpool and receive large quantities of horse manure and 'night soil' for spreading on their fields. At a later date Liverpool rubbish was also dumped alongside the canal in the Rimrose valley and you can still find old bottles and fragments of china there.

Leeds & Liverpool Canal boats were bigger than canal narrow boats because they were fourteen feet wide. Up to the 1930s they were either towed by a horse or a steam tug. You can see several surviving boats at the Boat Museum, Ellesmere Port. The passenger packets' holds were decked over and fitted out with first and second class cabins. They had two horses rather than one and the leading horse was ridden by a postilion in a red uniform who had a horn to alert other boats and waiting passengers of its approach. A service between Wigan and Liverpool started in 1774, and by 1827 the summer service (between 1 June and 1 October) was up to seven boats each way daily. The first left Crosby at 7.45 a.m., arriving at Liverpool at 9.15 a.m. and there were sailings from Liverpool at 4.00 p.m. and 7.00 p.m. This made it possible to commute to work on a regular basis. At Wigan, there were connecting boats to Manchester and as the timetable pointed out, this meant that passengers avoided the risk of travelling on the boisterous Mersey estuary and avoided 'the frequent accidents attendant on steam boats'. If you thought trouble on suburban transport was a new problem, Thomas Newte writing in 1791 reported that when he travelled on a packet boat, he witnessed 'much disorder and very improper conduct which must make these vehicles very unpleasant to females'.

The change to cheaper mass travel came on 24 July 1848, when a steam railway was opened between Waterloo and Southport. Two years later this was extended to Sandhills Junction to join up with an existing line, which terminated at Exchange station. This line had been discussed three years earlier and a committee was set up which was chaired by

The gaily painted Leeds & Liverpool boat *George* preserved at the Boat Museum, Ellesmere Port, is typical of the thousands of barges which passed down the canal through Crosby en route for Liverpool.

A Lancashire & Yorkshire Railway locomotive of the type used in the 1850s between Liverpool and Southport.

William Blundell. This body went on to place a Bill before Parliament to gain the necessary powers to build the railway. It was claimed that the proposed railway would give 'ready access to the rapidly expanding bathing places along the coast', and throw open the area 'for the building of villas and residences'. George Stephenson, the engineer who built that first main line between Liverpool and Manchester in 1830, was made responsible for the line to Southport – a much easier piece of engineering than the 1830 line.

The terminus at Waterloo was to the north of South Road and the present station. The Railway public house marks roughly where it was. The 'Railway' itself was probably built around the time of the opening of the station. The station was well equipped with a spacious ticket office and waiting room and a temporary refreshment hut – 'the cosy and cheerful purveyor of genuine Eccles cakes and other edibles'. At first there were only three trains a day to and from Southport. With the extension to Liverpool, this was increased to one an hour and, as the demand for travel increased, built up to a greater frequency and this has been maintained apart from a period of cut-backs in the 1960s. The three original locomotives – *Sefton*, *Formby* and *Blundell* – were supplied by Tayleur & Co. of Newton-le-Willows, which later became the famous Vulcan Foundry of engine builders. Plans of similar Tayleur-built engines survive in the archives of National Museums Liverpool and if you want an impression of what they were like, the nearest survivor is the famous *Lion* engine, which is on show at the Manchester Science Museum.

Steam locomotives were relegated to goods trains and the occasional through train in 1903 when the whole line was converted to electric traction. Since then, it has gone through three generations of EMUs (electrical multiple units). One of the second type has been preserved at the Tramway Museum at Birkenhead. The current trains which were first introduced in 1978 have just been renovated.

Crosby and Blundellsands (the order was later reversed) and Hightown were the other two original stations. The former was sited next to Mersey Road, which had a level crossing. The original stationmaster's house still stands to the north of the bridge. Seaforth and Litherland was added in 1850. Waterloo and Blundellsands and Crosby stations were moved and changed to their present layout in 1880-81. Hall Road was added in 1874 thanks to the determination of Joseph Gardner. Gardner was a rich timber merchant who lived at the north end of Blundellsands and resented the long walk to the station. The Lancashire & Yorkshire Railway told him after much pressure that there needed to be at least another five houses in his neighbourhood to justify building a station. So, as he was a wealthy man, he built another five at his own expense. The company gave in and built Hall Road station. During the Second World War, a train maintenance depot was set up there. Today this is unused. Hall Road was also the setting for the arrest of eight IRA men in February 1921. They had travelled from Seaforth to Hall Road to set fire to hay stacks at local farms as part of a reprisal against the brutality of English 'Black and Tans' auxiliary soldiers in Ireland.

All of our stations have lost their original wood and glass canopies over the platforms. At Waterloo an original canopy of the same kind fronts South Road along with the original covered staircase from the ticket office to the platform. Hall Road has its original brick buildings. Seaforth and Litherland has shrunk from four to two platforms. It was also the terminus of the Liverpool Overhead Railway from 1905 until 1956.

The railways once carried all the goods that now go by road and there were extensive goods sidings at Waterloo and Crosby and Blundellsands. Most of the building materials for constructing terraces and villas came by rail. Coal merchants brought their supplies in by rail often in their own wagons and all manner of miscellaneous goods were also distributed around the network. Passenger trains also carried small consignments and parcels. All those

Waterloo railway station was moved to its present site in 1880-81. In recent years it has been thoroughly modernized, but the original stairs and their canopy of cast iron, wood and glass still remain.

once busy sidings have been torn up, but you can see where they were once situated. At Waterloo, Kwik Save, the Royal Mail sorting office and the bus interchange occupy the old goods yard. At Blundellsands and Crosby, the goods sidings were on both sides of the tracks. There was a very long double loop on the east side, which extended as far as the end of St Anthony's Road. A builder's yard and Hall's Vehicle Services occupy much of the site. On the opposite side of the track, there were three more sidings and a goods office. It is now the station car park. Sandstone walls and a concrete gatepost mark its position.

Goods were carried locally in horse-drawn vehicles. There were also carters who delivered by horse and cart, and later lorry locally, and fetched and carried goods from Liverpool. One survival from this horse-drawn era is Armstrongs 'furniture removers and public carriers' who had a large depot in Victoria Road, Great Crosby. They used to run a daily parcel service between Liverpool, Crosby and Formby. This is now a shopfitter's workshop. They also had two furniture stores in St Luke's Road, one of which belongs to a plastics wholesaler and the other later one is part of Merchant Taylors' School for Girls where a loading hoist bay is still in situ.

In 1897, Liverpool received its first electric trams. Crosby and Waterloo still relied on horse buses, but their respective councils were anxious to see the new kind of road transport extended to their patch. Their intention was that some other body should supply this service and in 1898 they accepted an offer from the Liverpool Overhead Railway Co. offering to build and run an electric tramway from Seaforth Sands to Cooks Road at Crosby.

JAMES ARMSTRONG,
FURNITURE REMOVER & PUBLIC CARRIER
ROSE COTTAGE, VICTORIA, ROAD, GREAT CROSBY.

JAMES ARMSTRONG
PACKER
REMOVER OF FURNITURE
BY ROAD RAIL & SEA

JAMES ARMSTRONG
ESTABLISHED 1874
FURNITURE REMOVER.
GREAT CROSBY.

J. ARMSTRONG'S CARRYING CARTS leave CROSBY for LIVERPOOL every Morning at 9 30. Waterloo at 10 30. All Orders left before these hours in Crosby at his residence, or with Mr. COOK, Saddler, Liverpool Road, and in Waterloo, at Mr. LOWRY'S, Grocer, South Road, will have immediate attention.

CARTS leave Central Depot, Messrs. COFFEY BROTHERS, Provision Merchants, 40 Victoria Street, Liverpool, every Afternoon at 4 30. All Orders left before that time attended to same day.

All Charges Strictly Moderate.

Parcels and Goods Forwarded to all Parts

GOODS WAREHOUSED.

REMOVAL BY ROAD, RAIL OR SEA. DISTANCE NO OBJECT.

Complete Estimates and all particulars on application to—

JAMES ARMSTRONG, ROSE COTTAGE, VICTORIA ROAD, GREAT CROSBY.

BRANCH:— 2 DELTA ROAD, LITHERLAND.

Above: James Armstrong established his carting and furniture removal business in 1874. His main premises still stands in Victoria Road. The wing shown in this advertisement was built in 1883 and a second wing was added in 1896. Both have date stones.

Left: The last remains in situ of the Crosby tram system is the stump of one of the cast-iron columns that carried the overhead wires supplying the current. This is situated on Liverpool Road opposite St Peter and Paul's church. It was cast by Ham, Baker & Co. of Westminster.

The first experimental runs were made between Seaforth and the Five Lamps on 13 June 1900. There were teething problems with the unevenness of the track, but by October 1900 services started along the whole route. There were originally eight four-wheel double-deck trams with open tops supplied from Dick, Kerr & Co. of Preston and current was supplied to them from the LOR's power station via cables supported on cast-iron columns. It was a single line with passing loops at fourteen places, which were later reduced to ten. The service ran at ten-minute intervals for most of the day, and had carried over four and a half million passengers by 1919. The LOR's lease ended in 1925 and the company did not feel it was worth spending money to renew the ageing track and trams. Liverpool Corporation refused to take over the service, and on 23 December 1925 the two councils approached Whalley's Waterloo & Crosby Motor Services to supply an alternative bus service. This enterprising company which already ran a service between Crosby and Litherland managed to acquire enough second buses to start the new service by 1 January 1926 and the trams stopped. None of the trams survived. There are some photographs in the Local History Library, a fragment of one of the cast-iron columns carrying the overhead wires can be seen opposite St Peter and Paul's church on Liverpool Road and there is a possible waiting room on the allotments at Queensway.

Motorbus services started in Crosby in 1907 when the Lancashire & Yorkshire Railway started a service from Blundellsands and Crosby station to Thornton. This was not a success and the two buses were quickly withdrawn. This was the same year that W.A. Chatterton of South Road was offering horse-drawn wagonette excursions on Saturdays and Sundays to Lydiate, Sefton, Maghull and Childwall in the summer months. In the late 1920s, buses started to run through to Liverpool. They were started by William Slack's Nor' West Bus Services. In 1928 Ribble Services, which had started in 1919 and were expanding from their Preston base, acquired W & CMS and ran a service all the way from Southport to Liverpool via Crosby. The competition for Crosby fares increased with the arrival of the Ideal Bus Service and Imperial Motorways. Fares were reduced from a shilling return to between six pence and eight pence. Imperial which ran from the Duck Pond in Victoria Road charged the higher fare because their vehicles were luxury coaches. By the following year the latter two had dropped out, leaving Ribble to fight it out with Nor' West. In 1932 Ribble bought out its rival and had a monopoly of local services until they were taken over as part of the privatisation of bus services under the Thatcher government. Some of Ribble's distinctive PD3 Leyland buses of the 1950s have been preserved by private owners. The site of Ribble's Crosby bus station on Little Crosby Road (opened in 1938) is now a car repair centre.

Crosby had few firms that manufactured things. The largest was Kershaw's cotton mill, which was set up in about 1911 and closed in mid-1938. It specialised in weaving cotton and linen bags for products such as flour and stockinette and muslin for wrapping mutton and beef carcases. These found a ready market in Liverpool and district with the huge tonnage of meat being imported from Argentina, Australia and New Zealand and the live cattle brought over from Ireland to be slaughtered at Woodside lairage, Birkenhead. Its buildings were taken over by Littlewoods for its mail order business after the Second World War. They plan to quit the site in the next two years, after which the factory chimney and buildings will be pulled down to make way for houses. Then the sole remaining piece of evidence will be Kershaw Road, which leads off Endbutt Lane to the main entrance. There was another factory in nearby Musker Street, F.C. Blackwell (later became Simplex-Blaco Ltd) that made portable partitions for making up temporary ship's cabins for emigrants. There is a model of this patent design in the collection of Merseyside Maritime Museum. The firm later went on to specialize in the making of electrical conduit piping.

Above left: The chimney, which carried the waste gases from the boilers that provided the steam for a mill engine to drive the looms at Kershaw's cotton weaving factory, still stands at Littlewood's mail order centre. But for how long?

Above right: The late 1890s saw the building of large blocks of shops in Waterloo and Crosby. Crown Buildings was perhaps the most decorative with a mixture of mock-Tudor timbering, pebble-dash, turrets and Flemish gables. The latter make good use of the elaborate moulded bricks that were available from the brick makers around the Ruabon district of North Wales.

Thorougoods brewery in Queen Street, Waterloo, and Tower brewery, now under Sainsbury's car park, were both quite big establishments which have disappeared. Thorougood's letterhead showed a large building with their other breweries at Sefton and Burscough where the buildings still survive though not as breweries. The Queen Street brewery seems to have closed in about 1935. In 1888 Thomas Molyneux's Tower brewery, another large establishment in Great Crosby village, served twelve pubs around north Liverpool including the Crosby, Liverpool Road and the Hightown Hotel. A small derelict building behind the former International Marine Hotel on Crosby Road South may have also been a brewery. It has an oblong tapering ventilator of the kind so often found in breweries. Blundellsands Laundry in Mersey View was another factory-sized firm. Its building on Mersey View is still standing and is used by several different firms.

In the middle of the nineteenth century, most people's needs were either provided for at home or by small local firms. Skilled local craftsmen built and maintained transport and agricultural implements. The blacksmith not only shoed horses, he made a wide variety of metal items, from plough and cart components to wrought-iron gates. In 1888, there were four local blacksmith's shops. There are photographs of the one that used to be on the Liverpool Road side of the Liver Inn. It was the Liver Shoeing Forge owned by Rimmer & Dickinson in the 1930s and one of their account books is in the Village Museum at Little Crosby. The same museum has a wonderful collection of blacksmith's tools including a

Satterthwaite's oldest shop appears to be in South Road, complete with a wooden frontage and stained glass in the upper lights.

forge and bellows and a huge variety of special shaping tools such as swages and fullers. Little Crosby also still has its stone-built blacksmith's forge (though not working) at the Great Crosby end of the village street. The last local wheelwright was George Wharton who gave up in 1958 and whose workshop still stands on the other side of Little Crosby's street from the blacksmiths. Again, you will find typical wheelwright's tools in the Village Museum.

A mill driven by wind or water was another essential service in an agricultural area. There were four mills at different times in the two Crosbys. The tall brick tower of the last one built in 1814 still stands as a unique dwelling on Moor Lane. Some of the last of its machinery was rescued in 1971 and is in the National Museums Liverpool's reserve collections store.

Shops in the rural days were suppliers of basics. In 1854, Great Crosby and Waterloo had three provision dealers, one butcher, one draper, one tailor, three shoemakers, two saddlers, one wine merchant, three watchmakers, one stationer and more unusually one ink manufacturer. As the population increased, the number and range of the shops increased. By 1888, provision dealers had been renamed grocers and there were thirteen in Crosby and fifteen in Waterloo. The same increase was seen in the other kinds of shop: seven butchers in Crosby and eight in Waterloo, five and seven drapers respectively. Waterloo had a monopoly with six tailors, plus fourteen dressmakers with another four in Crosby. Between them there were ten wine merchants and five watchmakers. There were many

Thoroughgood's brewery in Queen Street, Waterloo, was the biggest local brewery and was a big establishment judging by the vignette on the firm's letterhead.

other specialised shops, including carvers and gilders, glass and china dealers, greengrocers, fancy repositories (the Victorian equivalent of our gift and card shops), fishmongers, florists, fruiterers, hosiers, ironmongers and tobacconists. There were also professionals offering services such as doctors, dentists, estate agents, architects, and two ventriloquists in Waterloo. There were none of the chain stores that are so familiar today. Independent suburban shops thrived in the late nineteenth century because real wages rose, and the price of food went down with the import of large amounts of cheap meat and grain after 1870. The mass production of manufactures – anything from textiles to china – also reduced their prices and put them within reach of more customers.

The first multiple stores to compete with these independent stores were those of the Co-operative Societies. There seems to have been at least four local branches of the Liverpool Co-op. By 1881, Co-ops had half a million members. In many places, they were followed by privately owned chains of shops which could purchase goods in bulk and undercut competitors by accepting low profit margins on a high turnover. These included Woolworths, which arrived from America in 1900. In their shops, every item for sale was at a fixed standard price. Boots the chemists were another example, they diversified from selling medicines to gifts, stationary and cosmetics as well as running a lending library of the latest novels. There were also Liverpool-based multiple stores such as Irvins the grocers and Blackledges the bakers, who both had several local stores. These included Blackledge's Oxford Road branch, which was until recently the Solid Wood furniture shop, and Irvins Crosby village branch, which is occupied by an opticians and a gent's outfitters. Satterthwaites, the local bakers, are a surviving example of a small chain of shops which started before the First World War.

The housing developments of the 1920s and 1930s were built with their own rows of essential shops. So, for example, there are rows of such shops on Oxford Road between Waterloo and Brighton Le Sands, on Brownmoor Lane, at the junction of Endbutt Lane and Liverpool Road and as an extension of College Road. Many are built in the same style with flat or sloped roofs behind brick-panelled parapets. Many of the basic shops have gone although greengrocers and newsagents seem to have survived better than grocers. However, the independents continue to survive but offering different services. We have a plentiful supply of hairdressers and takeaways and these have been joined by an increasing number of café bars and beauty salons.

FIVE

Institutions and Amenities

As Great Crosby and Waterloo expanded from the middle of the nineteenth century, they developed an increasing variety of institutions and amenities. By 1914, along with the hundreds of new villas, semis and terraces, there were new churches and chapels, new recreational facilities including pubs and sports clubs. There were also civic amenities such as parks and libraries run by the two district councils.

Waterloo and Great Crosby like many other new suburbs contained the homes of middle-class people who valued their own respectability and their status. Homes were seen not simply as a place to live but as a microcosm of Christian society. Father, the breadwinner, benignly ruled over his family, which might include servants and unmarried or widowed relatives. The emphasis was on polite behaviour, cleanliness, tidiness and 'good taste'. Most of the family's entertainments took place in the home. Parlour games, needle work, reading and making music usually with a piano were typical. Going to entertainments or eating outside the home were rare events unless it was in other friends' houses. Churches and chapels were the places for social contact as well as worship. Sunday was the key day for leisure because this was the only day when Father was not working. It included the ritual of dressing in best clothes, attending church, a roast Sunday lunch and an afternoon walk.

Before the mid-nineteenth century, Great Crosby had St Michael's chapel which was a dependency of the mother church of St Helen's, Sefton. This chapel was first recorded in 1564. The chapel was rebuilt in 1770 and was demolished in 1863 leaving the tower standing as a landmark for shipping. The latter was demolished about 1870. It used to stand in the car park behind Barclays Bank. The bricks from the tower were recycled to help build St Luke's School for Boys, which was opened in 1871. When that was demolished in 1975 some of the bricks and a stone lintel were used to build a seat at the front of St Luke's church. St Michael's communion silver has been passed on to its successor. St Michael's also had a healing well which is still marked by a cross on a stone plinth in the Islington car park. As water and wells were sacred places for the Romano-British people, perhaps this was a pagan place of worship before the establishment of Christianity.

Leisure time was very limited for all but the rich before the nineteenth century, and the only days off were Sundays and Holy Days. Michaelmas, celebrating St Michael and All Angels on 29 September, was clearly important in Great Crosby. It was linked to a Goose Feast. Goose dinners were offered at local inns and there was a two-day fair with stalls and amusements.

Above: The plain exterior of St John's, Waterloo (1864-65) hides a splendid hammer-beam roof and some very good stained glass in lancet windows. The cost of repairs to one of the oldest churches has threatened it with demolition.

Right: Christchurch, Waterloo (1891-94) has a magnificent cathedral-sized interior. Though made redundant for services, Christchurch has been conserved and is opened for local history days.

Christchurch National School in Great Georges Road was an early school dating back to 1842 and has a fine stone plaque with elaborate Victorian lettering.

Many local people remained faithful to the Catholic faith after Henry VIII's Reformation. At first, they were persecuted and had to worship in secret. A plaque in Moorside park commemorates Laurence Johnson of Moorside Farm who became a Catholic priest in 1577 and was executed at Tyburn in 1582. After the Restoration of Charles II in 1660, they achieved a measure of toleration, but were barred from voting, public office and the universities until 1829. The Harkirk chapel in the woods of Little Crosby Hall marks a Catholic burial ground, which was in use between 1610 and 1753. The chapel itself dates from 1889 and incorporates some of the seventeenth-century gravestones in its walls.

St Luke's was not the first new church in the area. In 1815, Sir John Gladstone, one of the first of the rich Liverpool merchants to move north out of Liverpool to his new Georgian mansion of Seaforth Hall, did not like the services at Sefton church and built his own church dedicated to St Thomas at Seaforth. Its brick walls were covered with stucco and painted white in the same fashion as the Royal Hotel and Marine Crescent. Unfortunately, in 1980 it was demolished. The later parish hall is the church now.

The oldest surviving Anglican church in Waterloo, St John's of 1864, is also under threat because of the need for extensive repairs. The Independent Chapel, East Street, Waterloo was the first local non-conformist place of worship and was also demolished in the 1980s, but not before it had been converted to other uses including a drill hall – hence the name of the pub next door, the Volunteer Canteen.

As Great Crosby and Waterloo grew rapidly from the 1870s, further churches and more denominations were added. Some churches started as small or even temporary structures, which were later replaced. For example, the present Catholic church of St Peter and St Paul replaced a chapel that went back to 1826. Before the present church was opened in 1874, the congregation of St Nicholas' church, Blundellsands, worshipped in a 'tin tabernacle' – a prefabricated building clad in corrugated iron. Hundreds of these church kits assembled by firms such as Mortons of Garston were exported to all parts of the British Empire. St Michael's, Blundellsands, started in a 'tin tabernacle' in 1907, and was replaced in 1931.

Boundary Cottage (1842), Little Crosby Road, once a school for Catholic children and later a drill hall for the Artillery Volunteers.

Fifteen major churches were built in Great Crosby, Waterloo and Seaforth between 1874 and 1900. In addition, Catholic convents were established at Seafield House (later moved to what is now the Sacred Heart School), Nazareth House and Park House and the Christian Brothers ran St Mary's College at Claremont House.

The great influx of middle-class families also saw the expansion of educational facilities. Merchant Taylors' School had never fulfilled its potential before the nineteenth century. Its scholars were often absent to attend to farming jobs. The headmaster was able to combine teaching with acting as curate at St Michael's and running a smallholding. Anthony Halsall, who was appointed headmaster in 1730, is remembered in a memorial plaque in Sefton church and his sister Catherine left money in 1758 to establish the Halsall School for Girls. From the 1850s, under the guidance the Revd John Bernard, Merchant Taylors' grew in size, and in 1878 it moved to its present building. Its Gothic architecture and its tall central tower reflected its new status. In 1883, the original seventeenth-century building became part of the new Merchant Taylor's School for Girls.

Those in government in the early nineteenth century often doubted the wisdom of universal education because of the risk that the working classes might get above themselves and undermine the status quo. There was no compulsory education until 1870 and even so, only the poorest families were exempt from fees. In 1833, the government did provide a grant to church-based education societies to build more schools and the National Society built a school in Great Crosby in the 1820s and another in Waterloo in 1842. The latter building still survives in Great Georges Road. The Great Crosby School, which stood in

St Mary's College was founded in 1919 in the grounds of Claremont House, an Italianate-style villa, possibly dating to the 1860s with ornamental cast-iron gateposts.

The Marine at the bottom of South Road was marked on the 1850 Ordnance Survey map as the Bath Hotel. The frontage was modernized in the 1930s to give it an Art Deco look with steel-framed windows and the zig-zag mouldings. The figurehead of a mermaid has unfortunately disappeared.

the front of St Luke's church, had declined by the 1840s and was revived in 1864 on the site of the old St Michael's chapel. William Blundell's school for Catholic children in Little and Great Crosby also opened in 1842. After 1859 there were separate schools in the two parishes and it became a drill hall for the Artillery Volunteers and then Boundary Cottage. The introduction of compulsory schooling also introduced a new problem of truancy. By 1880, the problem of truanting 'street Arabs' was so bad in Liverpool that a special truant school was built at Hightown to take away the worst offenders from their environment and try to reform them with a harsh regime of schooling and gardening. The school was demolished in 1962, but School Road is a reminder of its existence.

Educational facilities continued to expand for the rest of the nineteenth and into the twentieth century. For example, between 1894 and 1936 Waterloo Council built six elementary schools and two secondary schools including Waterloo Grammar School on Cambridge Road. Its current use as an adult education centre reflected the change to comprehensive education in the early 1970s. As the population has begun to decrease, recent years have seen the closure of well-loved schools such as Rawson Road Primary School in Seaforth, which was established in 1911.

Private education flourished in the area. As early as 1853 Henry Grazebrook wrote that the only important thing about Seaforth was that it provided 'several human menageries or training establishments for young females'. By the end of the nineteenth century, local directories show that young ladies were being educated in schools such as the Blankenburg Ladies School in Coronation Road or the Norma School at 17 Norma Road or the Detmold College for Girls at 34 Brooke Road and the Girls High School at 14 Wellington Street. Streatham House, a late-comer, was founded by Violet and Daisy Harvey in 1925 with only six pupils, and is still going strong. Boys schools included Blundellsands House, a large Victorian villa on Burbo Bank Road which was replaced by an Art Deco set of flats in the 1930s, and St Mary's College for Catholics which was started at a similar dwelling, Claremont, on Liverpool Road in 1919.

Many middle-class people were ambivalent about public houses with their connotations of working-class drunkenness. Temperance was a national issue because drunkenness was perceived as a huge social evil. In 1850 at the start of the era of local growth, there were two respectable hotels in Waterloo, a Total Abstinence Hotel where the present Crosby Hotel stands, the Liver, George and Ship Victory inns and several beerhouses. The latter were licensed to sell only beer and were introduced in 1830 as an antidote to the widespread and pernicious habit of drinking spirits. Beer was seen as a healthy and affordable alternative to gin. For example in 1888, East Street, Waterloo, had two beerhouses, the A1 at Lloyds and the Canteen Vaults. The latter is still with us as the Volunteer Canteen. Over the following century, public houses not only grew in number, but the better-class ones were called hotels even though they might not provide accommodation. They provided their clientele with a choice of bars including a public bar, a lounge with waitress service, a billiards room, and a take-out counter. They were lavishly appointed with fine panelling and stained glass. The well-loved Volunteer Canteen and the Crow's Nest still retain much of their original furnishings and club-like atmosphere. The Crow's Nest even has 'an honours list' of Old Crows going up to 1973 in the Snug. Where else?

Pubs grew larger and the grander ones such as the George, the Brooke, the Endbutt and the Seaforth Arms were made to look like half-timbered manor houses or, in the case of the Seaforth, a late seventeenth-century baroque mansion. Both the Brooke and the Endbutt were next to large new developments of semi-detached houses. The Blundellsands

The Blundellsands Hotel was once at the heart of local social life. Many regret its conversion into flats. The 1890s design owed much to Norman Shaw, with contrasting red brick and yellow sandstone bands and quoins, bays, spindly chimneys and mock battlements – a baronial hall indeed.

Hotel was another large establishment which was a proper hotel and a social centre for hosting dinners, balls and wedding receptions.

Apart from tennis, archery, croquet and possibly cycling after the 1890s, most local sports were for men. Organised local ball games began to be established in the last two decades of the nineteenth century. In earlier times, rural pastimes such as coursing, bull baiting and cock fighting were common. Gentlemen like the Blundells would also shoot game birds. There was also a small racecourse on Great Crosby Marsh laid out in 1654 with a viewing area near Stanfield House on Liverpool Road. The Village Museum has a case with two fighting cocks wearing spurs, which suggests that cock fighting probably went on locally into the nineteenth century.

Public schools promoted the playing of sports such as rugby and cricket as part of a gentleman's education. Their popularity led to the foundation of clubs for amateur sportsmen such as the Waterloo Rugby Football Club and the Northern Cricket Club.

Waterloo started as an offshoot of a winning Merchant Taylor's team in 1882, which played on an informal pitch off the Serpentine. In 1884 the club moved to a pitch on Manley Road, Waterloo. This was one of several moves including using the playing field vacated at Haigh Road by the Northern Cricket Club in 1907. The present ground at St Anthony's Road, Blundellsands, was bought in 1919 as a memorial to the fifty-one members of the club who lost their lives in the First World War. The original part of the

The Northern Cricket Club still has its original 1907 pavilion and a pitch good enough for the Lancashire First team squad to practice on at the start of the 2005 season. Dominic Cork was batting here and went on to make a century.

club's buildings has a comprehensive collection of framed photographs of their First teams going back to 1884 when shorts were longer and the jerseys had stripes.

The Northern Cricket Club started at Seaforth in 1859 close to Rawson Road and moved to Waterloo Park in 1879. In 1907 they moved to Moor Park. The pavilion is still the original although with extensions, and it still retains the bell presented to them by their chairman Robert Moss in 1879. The Waterloo Cricket Club started as the Norma Cricket Club playing on waste ground on Norma Road They then moved to a ground known as Bellman's Field behind St Mary's church, Waterloo Park, and moved to Chesterfield Road in 1934. This ground was unfortunately sold for housing in the 1980s.

The Bootle Almanack for 1879 listed football clubs at Crosby Road North, Waterloo, and at Blundellsands near the station. Bellman's Field was also let for tennis, bowls and football. Marine Football Club, which had been founded at the Marine Hotel, Waterloo, played there until they moved to their present ground on College Road in 1904. The lower end of this field (next to the railway) was used by the boys of Blundellsands House and is marked by the present Crossender Road.

Tennis and archery were popular because they were sports in which both sexes could take part and thus provided an opportunity for young men and women to meet. There were large houses with their own courts such as St Luke's vicarage and there were also clubs. The Blundellsands Lawn Tennis Club is probably the oldest and was founded in

Waterloo Gymnasium,

OLIVE ROAD (ADJOINING THE STATION).

CLASSES.

LADIES'....Mondays and Thursdays ....at 2 30 p.m.
GIRLS' ....Wednesdays and Saturdays....at 2 15 „
BOYS' .... do do ...at 3 45 „

Principal and Instructress - - - Miss DAVIES.

☞ *Terms on Application.* ☜

Gentlemen's Gymnasium Club.

Mondays, Wednesdays and Saturdays at 7 p.m.

Instructor - Mr. HENRY SMITH
(OF THE LIVERPOOL AND WARRINGTON GYMNASIA).

Terms—Entrance Fee, 5/-; Annual Subscription, £1 1/-.

To be Let,

FOR

Public Meetings, Concerts, Balls,

&c.

The Large Gymnasium Hall (Seating 600), with Supper
Room, Dressing Rooms, Kitchen, &c.

Apply on the Premises, or at 19 Church Road, Waterloo.

Left: The Kingsway Christian Centre started as a gymnasium as advertised here in 1888 and later became a cinema, then a theatre and then back to a cinema.

Below: The Palladium Cinema, Seaforth Road, has a Classical frontage with a pediment and swags of fruit and flowers all in moulded brick.

1880 as an offshoot of an existing archery club. In the early twentieth century, the local councils provided less exclusive sporting facilities for sports like tennis and bowls in the newly established parks. Churches also provided sports facilities. For example, in the 1930s St Luke's Fellowship organised gymnastic classes, athletics, netball, tennis and ladies' hockey. Today, St John's parish hall contains a magnificent sporting relic in the shape of a full-size Victorian billiard table complete with all its equipment and scoreboards.

While the football and other sports clubs attracted clerks and other lower middle-class professionals, those with more money and status turned to sports with a higher social cachet such as golf and yachting. West Lancashire Golf Club was established in the sand dunes to the north of Blundellsands in 1873. It was originally laid out on both sides of the railway, but the northern section was later taken for houses and the Waterloo Rugby Club's pitches. Rather more enlightened than some golf clubs, West Lancs had a separate ladies' club with their own course by 1884 and an Artisans' club in 1921. Blundellsands Sailing Club was established about 1891 when it was reported the club was moving to a club house at Hightown. Blundellsands continues today with a fleet of cruising yachts. One of their Tyrer class dinghies is preserved at the Maritime Museum. The opening of the Crosby Marina in 1973 made for safer dinghy racing and opened up the sport to a wider range of people.

Apart from sports clubs, the district also supported and continues to support a wide range of music, drama and other leisure activities such as Lucilla Drama group with its own premises in Victoria Road, Great Crosby, the Crosby Gilbert and Sullivan Society or the Crosby Symphony Orchestra. By the time of Queen Victoria's death in 1901, the trend to more passive forms of leisure activity was underway. Instead of playing sport, you could watch the growing number of professional matches. Instead of playing the piano, you could listen to music on a gramophone and instead of attending a play you could watch moving pictures at the cinema. The first two cinemas were the Bijou (in the old chapel next to the Volunteer Canteen) and the Winter Gardens in Church Street. This survives as the Kingsway Christian Fellowship. It had been built as a gymnasium in the 1870s and in the 1920s was turned into a theatre. Lathom Hall in Seaforth was a cinema between 1912 and 1916 and the Palladium, also in Seaforth and which opened in 1913, survives as a gym, as does the once up-market Regent opened in 1920 on Liverpool Road, Great Crosby. The Queen's also opened in 1913 and was turned into a furniture store on South Road in 1960 and the Corona (1920) in College Road and the Stella (1920) in Seaforth Road have both been demolished. Only the Plaza opened in 1939 remains as a working cinema. Such was the devastating effect of television on the cinemas in the 1960s.

Local administration developed along with the other institutions that turned Great Crosby and Waterloo-with-Seaforth into an urban area. The councils remained separate until their merger in 1936. Their early priorities were the supply of basic services. Bit by bit they acquired powers to extend their responsibilities. Voluntary fire brigades were established at Waterloo in the 1880s and at Great Crosby in 1894. Waterloo's original station survives as the Citizen's Advice Bureau in York Street. Behind the present fire station on Crosby Road North is a splendid collection of old fire engines belonging to the Merseyside Fire Museum. The Waterloo–with-Seaforth Local Board of Health was set up in 1856 and built itself offices on Church Road in 1862, which were extended when the Board was converted into an Urban District Council in 1893. The Great Crosby equivalent took over the Alexandra Assembly Rooms, which had been built as a private venture in 1883. This again provided a meeting space for the council, offices and accommodation for dances and concerts.

The original Waterloo Voluntary Fire Brigade's station is still there in York Street next to the Town Hall, but is now the Citizens Advice Bureau.

The original Waterloo library and museum still stands unused in Church Road and its collection of stuffed birds lies in store in Bootle.

Coronation Park boating lake remains a popular venue for model boat builders and many users, including the local ducks.

Parks were another new feature. The Blundells donated three and a half acres of land for a recreation ground off Thorpe's Lane, which became Coronation Park in 1902. This was followed by Alexandra Park. Waterloo Council, not to be outdone, developed Victoria Park in 1902 and Potter's Barn in 1908 and other green spaces followed. One of the least known is the donation by F.N. Blundell of Sniggery Wood in 1935. Snigs was an old name for eels and a series of depressions in the wood suggests that there were once fish ponds here. Two libraries followed at College Road in 1905 and Church Road in 1908. Both were funded by grants from the American philanthropist, Andrew Carnegie. Commercial libraries also flourished because public libraries tended to stock worthy volumes and not the latest romances and thrillers. Sugden's in South Road offered the latest novels for four pence halfpenny a week before 1914.

The Waterloo Library also contained a small museum, which is all but forgotten. The building was damaged in the Second World War and replaced in 1968. On the first floor is a computer suite named the Echalaz Room. This used to house wonderful dioramas of birds and animals, which came from the original museum. They were all shot by Lt-Col. C.T. Echalaz who retired from the Indian Army to Blundellsands in 1886. He had them stuffed and mounted in realistic scenes by a taxidermist in Southport. He donated them in the hope that they 'might prove a valuable adjunct to the Carnegie Library'. They have deteriorated over the years and are stored awaiting conservation. His name was carved over the entrance to the museum in Church Road and he also had a fine catalogue published which can be found in the Local History section.

Crosby's rich mix of building materials and styles is typified by the buildings at the northern end of Beach Lawn, Waterloo – stucco with a touch of Gothic contrasting with next door's bay bright two-coloured brickwork.

Part Two

The Building Materials of Great Crosby and District

This section deals with the different types of materials that have been used to make buildings in Crosby over the centuries – timber, stone, slate, brick, glass, iron, steel and concrete. These are roughly in chronological order. But there are huge overlaps. For example, we still use wood extensively today in the roof structure of modern domestic dwellings and for fittings such as window frames. As we have seen in the earlier chapters, Great Crosby and most of the district were transformed in the late nineteenth century from a rural area to a suburb of Liverpool. The evidence for the earlier phase of timber houses has to be sought in examples outside our boundaries. Early stone buildings do survive, especially at Little Crosby. Bricks were once all made locally. The arrival of the railway opened up the opportunity of bringing in cheaper mass-produced bricks from other areas. Welsh slate became the favoured roofing material in the nineteenth century, replacing thatch or sandstone flags. In the late twentieth century, some large Victorian villas have been demolished to make way for flats or groups of smaller houses, and Waterloo and Seaforth have seen the building of steel and concrete-framed towers blocks and office buildings. All these are part of the wealth of material evidence of how Crosby developed, and they often come with some surprises.

There were other uses for these materials. Stone was often carved with inscriptions which range from gravestones and memorials to date stones on buildings. Clay in its plastic state can be finely moulded and there are many examples of ornamental brickwork here in Crosby. In the same way, cast iron can be poured into moulds and take on intricate detail as well as providing building strength in columns and beams. Signs of all kinds are examined in the final chapter and these were often placed high up on buildings and as a result are largely ignored by pedestrians and car drivers at ground level. Look up and you will see a different Crosby, full of curiosities.

SIX
Timber

Aside from naturally formed caves, timber was the main building material for our early ancestors' homes. No evidence exists of the earliest dwellings, but we know they were cutting down trees. This is because the petrified tree stumps of prehistoric trees have been exposed in nineteenth-century excavations in Crosby. Neolithic man felled trees for fuel, to build and above all to make space for his agriculture. The clearing of trees continued down the centuries. By the time of the compilation of the Domesday Book, it has been estimated that woods covered about quarter of the area of Merseyside. Today, it is only about four per cent and much of this is late nineteenth- and twentieth-century plantations of pines concentrated on the coast to the north of Formby. Initiatives such as the Mersey Forest tree-planting scheme are increasing the number of trees again. But these and those that line the streets of Great Crosby and Blundellsands are amenities and not for timber production. Waterloo seems to have lost many of its street trees, for example on South Road and St John's Road. There are woods around the parks of the two local halls at Little Crosby and Ince Blundell and some isolated woods such as Sniggery and Flea Moss woods to the north, but most if not all of their trees were planted in the nineteenth century as well.

The oldest evidence of local timber housing is an aerial photograph of a circular Romano-British settlement to the north of Little Crosby. This has not been excavated but it is a fair guess that this would have had a circular fence guarding a circular wooden hut. The hut would have been constructed with a low wall of stakes with roof timbers attached to them to form a cone-shaped framework. Light hazel rods were bent round these to make purlins to which bundles of straw could be tied to form a roof. The wall spaces would be filled with woven hazel rods, which were then covered with a mixture of clay, animal dung and plenty of straw. When dry, this 'wattle and daub' recipe made a substantial wall. The recent exhibition at the Museum of Liverpool Life about the Romans in the North West of England had a reconstruction of one of these huts complete with furnishings, a fire and an appropriately dressed actor.

All the wood needed for such a dwelling was of a small section. Coppicing was a way of managing trees so that small diameter poles could be harvested at regular intervals. Coppice wood could be used for fuel or charcoal making or woodland crafts such as making hurdles or baskets. Husbanding trees was important not only for the wood but in this area for stopping drifting sand and soil erosion. Local landowners such as the Blundells managed their woods and planted new trees and punished anyone who stole wood. In 1708, Nicholas Blundell discovered that Richard Ainsworth his ploughman had stolen

This is a reconstruction of a circular Romano-British hut at the Museum of Liverpool Life. The Romano-British sites identified by aerial photography in the district may have looked like this when they were occupied.

wooden boards among other things. Blundell took him to the Assizes at Lancaster to be tried for robbery where he was barbarously punished by being branded on the hand.

The Anglo-Saxons introduced oblong timber-framed houses and archaeologists have reconstructed some at West Stow in Suffolk from information gained from digs. They were much the same size as their round predecessors and it is likely that the ordinary peasant's huts in our area were similar. Some time in the Middle Ages, and no one can be sure, a special kind of timber framing known as crucks, which economised on timber, was introduced. Crucks were large, naturally curved timbers, which were set upright in pairs. They were stabilised by cross pieces and linked together by horizontal beams. The outer walls were filled with panels of woven hazel and plastered with daub and the roof was thatched. Rye straw was popular in Lancashire as a roofing material, and could last up to thirty years. Marshy areas also grew reeds, which made a more durable thatching material. It is likely that many of the small farms of our area were built in this way. Not one has survived. The last was Pinfold Cottage (formerly Home Farm), on Cooks Road, which stood where Pinfold Court is now. It was demolished in 1961 but not before a detailed plan was drawn. Crucks have survived in houses on the periphery of Crosby. Most of them are concealed by later brick exteriors, and include Homer Green Farm in Sefton, the Cross Barn in Ince Blundell and six cottages in Formby.

The Village pub was built partly in mock-Tudor style, which drew on the styles of sixteenth- and seventeenth-century timber-framed houses in the North West.

The upper storey of the Village includes a number of carved busts such as this bearded Tudor gentleman.

Only basic tools were needed for building timber-framed houses. Oak was the favoured wood because this could be split into suitable baulks using wedges and a large mallet known as a beetle. Unlike cutting the wood with a saw, splitting preserved the strength of the grain and did not cut through wood cells, which allowed rot in. Timbers could be trued up and smoothed with a broad axe and an adze. The latter has a horizontal blade and in the right hands can trim and smooth wood with great precision. Chisels would be used to make joints and a drawknife would be employed for fashioning pegs for fastening the frame together. You can see all these old-fashioned tools in the Village Museum, Little Crosby. Many timber-framed houses were replaced by stone or brick ones, but you can sometimes see a stone base to a brick house which indicates that it has replaced a wooden one. There were distinctive styles of timber framing according to the region and the great timber-framed houses of the North West which date from the late fifteenth to the early seventeenth century were ostentatious. Their timbers were coated with pitch and the infilling of lath and plaster was whitewashed, which achieved the classic black and white Tudor style. Surviving examples include Speke Hall and Rufford Old Hall. Lydiate Hall and Sefton Hall were built to the same fashion, but both unfortunately have been demolished. So, while there was no such example within Crosby, this distinctive North Western design was revived in the late nineteenth century for many of the new houses in the district.

The sea could supplement local supplies of timber. Shipwrecks, common along this coast, were valuable not only for the cargoes but for the hull of the vessel as well. If it could not be salvaged, it would be broken up and its timbers re-used. One of the farm buildings at the Village Museum is believed to have been built with ship's timbers. The other way the sea helped was through the large-scale import of timber from abroad. By the early 1800s, Liverpool had became a major importer of wood, especially from Canada. In 1832, a special timber-importing dock, Brunswick Dock, was opened and this was followed by a second one, Canada Dock, in 1858 and later on a large area of the Seaforth shore was devoted to timber storage. While much of this wood was sold for use elsewhere, imported woods such as pitch pine can be found in the woodwork of nineteenth-century homes often in extravagantly large pieces. For example, the purlins of the roofs of Claremont Terrace, Victoria Road, Great Crosby measure a massive fifteen inches by five inches.

Fashions in architecture, as with so many other things, start with the rich and percolate down to the rest of us. The 1870s saw the rise of architects such as Norman Shaw who specialised in providing the wealthy with new country houses. Shaw and other contemporaries saw merit in reviving old English styles of vernacular architecture. As we have already observed, much of the inspiration came from the rural buildings in the Home Counties. Some went for making authentic copies and trying to revive the hand-made products of earlier times. Others deployed many different materials, often juxtaposing different styles and materials and developing a new architectural language. Timber-framed Elizabethan and Jacobean houses were one style, which became popular. Unlike the originals, the black and white timber framing was not part of the structure. Instead the timbers were applied only to the front of the building and quite often only to the first storey. It was a fashion taken up by the idealistic entrepreneurs who developed improved housing for their workers. Port Sunlight, which was developed by William Hesketh Lever (later the 1st Viscount Leverhulme) from 1888, has many examples of this combination. Most of the work was commissioned from local architects who doubtless went on to build similar houses around Merseyside. While mock-Tudor was found up and down the country, local houses took on some of the decorative features of the North Western originals such as a herringbone pattern of timbers, curved braces or quatrefoils between the main verticals.

There are many diluted examples of mock-Tudor among local houses. Most of this type of decoration is confined to the first-floor elevations. Number 54 Kimberley Drive is among the most authentic, with two different types of quatrefoil (four-lobed) patterns.

The earliest example of mock-Tudor is 1 Agnes Road next to Blundellsands station. This has a brick and stone ground floor, bearing the Blundell coat of arms and the date 1866. The front and the two side gables are decorated. It has a combination of crossed and curved braces, which make a pleasing pattern. The bargeboards are made more interesting by being shaped and braced by a horizontal cross-beam with a king post and two side braces. This is very early for a mock-Tudor house. Number 28 Blundellsands Road West (opposite 1 Agnes Road) is another good example of elaborate black and white decoration. The main gable contains a projecting oriel window, which was another common feature on Tudor houses, framed by curved braces. Other good examples are to be found in Warren Road, Moor Park and in Kimberley and Coronation Drives. Number 54 Kimberley Drive has authentic North Western-style quatrefoils, while 15 and 17 Coronation Drive have designs, which though not authentic, add interest to their twin gables.

We find simplified versions of mock-Tudor in many other parts of Crosby and Waterloo. Many have a nominal pattern of timbers in their front gables. This is especially true of the large numbers of semi-detached houses built between the two world wars. The Winchester Avenue to Brooke Road East set of avenues are lined with semi-detached houses, and some have mock-Tudor gables and some do not. This was part of the appeal of such houses to the first residents. While they were all slightly different, yet they were not so different to stand out from the rest. Urban cosiness with nostalgic hints from bygone Merrie England was an essential constituent of their appeal.

These are just a few of the varieties of the residual mock-Tudor timberwork found on the gables of local twentieth-century homes. All these happen to be in Cooks Road.

The most spectacular examples of mock-Tudor timberwork which approach the quality of the well known ones in the centre of Chester are to be found at the heart of Great Crosby village at the junction of Moor Lane and Liverpool Road. Looking at old photographs of this area before 1900, you see a rather nondescript set of shops without any prestigious-looking buildings. Then in 1901 a group of buildings was added. The Moor Lane end, which was built as a bank and is now the Village Bar, has a three-gabled half-timbered upper section with carved pilasters with Jacobean strapwork topped by four carved busts. Just down the street Crown Buildings was built shortly afterwards in 1904 with two Flemish gables and two half-timbered gables. It was not until 1929 that the George Hotel on the opposite side of the street was rebuilt from a modest establishment into a large 'Roadhouse' style of hostelry. As the *Crosby Herald* reported in 1928, the existing building was over 100 years old and totally inadequate. The architect Mr R. Metcalfe was commissioned by Threlfall's, the Liverpool brewers, to build a commodious

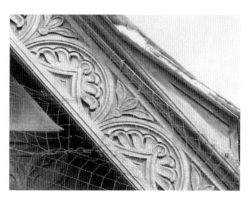

Fretted bargeboards and carved work were another form of timber decoration. From left to right and from top to bottom: 27 Cooks Road; carved oak leaves on the bargeboards of the Endbutt Hotel; a carved bracket supporting the projecting gable of the Birkey Hotel; Cottage Farm, Little Crosby; spandrels on the side door of the Brooke Hotel with grotesque dolphins and the monogram of Threlfall's, the owners; a more geometrical pattern copied from Tudor sources on the bargeboards of the George Hotel.

premises in the Elizabethan style. Only the upper storey of the corner gable is half-timbered. There is an oriel window and carved beams and bargeboards, and the two side timbers are finished off with massive bosses carved with bunches of grapes and vine leaves. Threlfalls had also transformed the Brooke Hotel in 1922 and the Endbutt probably in 1923. Both exhibit many of the same fine carved work and it is likely that Metcalfe also designed these two re-buildings. However they are by no means identical. The Endbutt has three gables and a projecting porch, which has some fine carvings of oak leaves and acorns on the lower crossbeam. The Brooke has one large central gable and a smaller one to its right. Again the detailed carving on the horizontal beams is well executed and there is a fine pair of dolphins on the lintel over the old Jug and Bottle entrance. The Birkey on Cooks Road was another Threlfalls pub that has received a mock-Tudor make-over, but the detailing is nowhere as good as the others and the ground floor is built of brick and not stone. This suggests that it was probably a later rebuilding. Some of the finest pieces of timber joinery work are to be found in the roofs of local churches. St John's, Waterloo, and the United Reformed Church in Eshe Road have hammer beam roofs spanning the entire width of their naves. They are superb pieces of engineering in timber, and reminiscent, though less decorative, of one of London's secular medieval halls, which just happens to be called Crosby Hall. This has a Crosby connection because one of the architects responsible for saving it from demolition and moving it from the City to Cheyne Walk, Chelsea, was William Caroe. He was the son of the Danish consul and corn merchant who lived at Holmesdale, Blundellsands. He was primarily a church architect and some of his fine woodwork designs can be seen in the organ case of St Nicholas, Blundellsands.

Smaller buildings were and still are constructed from timber. Many of us have garden sheds and summer houses, which come prefabricated from the suppliers such as B&Q or the Shed Shop in Bootle. In the early 1900s John Dean, who was a local joiner, builder, plumber and decorator, advertised his rustic summer houses, shelters, motor garages and sports pavilions in the local directories. His workshop was at 55 and 57 Alexandra Road, which is Cheesman's glass workshop now. Many local sports pavilions were built of wood. That of the Northern Cricket Club dates from 1907 and is constructed with overlapping boards (clapboard) a common method of building rural cottages in Essex. Marine Football Club's tea room looks as if it was one of the original club buildings. Wood was also used for small workshops and offices. Crosby Memorials has such a building on the corner of Liverpool Road and St Luke's Road. Though partly covered in modern plastic sheeting, it probably dates back to the 1920s when W.H. Hastings had the business. Timber buildings had the advantage that they could be taken down and moved, and one of the huts on the Queensway allotments has surely been moved from another location. According to one local resident it was moved from the Five Lamps where it did duty as a tram shelter. Unlike North America where timber houses are the norm, timber homes were rare in twentieth-century England. The small bungalows promoted by the *Daily Mail* in their Ideal Home Exhibitions (first started in 1908) were popular as low-cost houses or as seaside holiday homes in the 1920s and 1930s. There used to be quite a number of such holiday bungalows in the sand dunes at Hightown. One possible survivor of this type is 'Four Winds' on Green Lane, Thornton.

Present-day houses still require timber. The roof structure is invariably made of wood, as are the internal framing for walls and doors and window frames. Many houses have replaced their original doors with new ones made from plastic or tropical hardwood. The same is true for most window frames. These change the appearance of the house and it is very difficult to find many local houses with their original features.

The magnificent carpentry supporting the Cumbrian slate roof of the United Reformed church on Eshe Road.

Fine oak carving can be found in many local churches. Some of the best can be found in the organ case of St Nicholas, Blundellsands. It was designed by W.D. Caroe, a church architect who was brought up at Holmesdale, Blundellsands. He was also responsible for the restoration of the district's mother church, St Helen's, at Sefton.

Wooden porches are an attractive decorative as well as functional feature in a coastal area such as ours: from left to right and from top to bottom: a Gothic touch on a villa of the 1870s on Blundellsands Road West; a porch on an 1880s semi-detached house on Regent Road, Great Crosby, with stained-glass panels and a finial of Ruabon brick; lead-roofed porch with a Gothic front door on one of the houses of Mersey View Terrace of 1822-23; and a post–1900 detached house in Victoria Road, Great Crosby, with a touch of the Art Nouveau about it. This pattern can be seen on other houses of this period in Crosby such as those on Queen's Road, Great Crosby.

Above left: An echo of mock–Tudor timber decoration can still be found in some more recent buildings such as these flats on Merrilocks Road.

Above right: John Dean was a maker of all kinds of wooden buildings as can be seen from his advertisement of 1913.

Left: This attractive wooden building, which serves an allotment shop at Queensway, has clearly been moved from elsewhere. One local resident believes it was the tram shelter from the Five Lamps, Waterloo.

Above left: The attractive herringbone framing of the outer door of 53 Brooke Road east is presumably original.

Above right: The prefabricated wood panel structure of the new flats building on the site of Hepburn's Garage, Bridge Road, Brighton Le Sands.

In the case of sash windows with their small divided panes, new picture windows look completely out of character. However, there are still homes which retain their original features. The semi-detached inter-war house at 53 Brooke Road East still retains its original front doors with herringbone wooden framing, while none of neighbours do. Some houses retain wooden features such as decorative bargeboards like those on Boundary Cottage, Little Crosby Road and Cottage Farm, Virgins Lane. Others have pretty wooden features such as wooden porches and balconies. And to show that wood is by no means out-dated for new buildings, it is worth noting that the new building at Sacred Heart School has exterior wood panelling and the new flats being built on the site of Hepburn's garage on Bridge Road are being constructed from prefabricated wooden panels.

SEVEN
Stone and Slate

There are outcrops of stone near Great Crosby and Waterloo, and plenty of buildings use stone in their structure. Sandstone is the most common, and is made up of sand grains, which are tiny particles of quartz, bound together by a natural cement. Our local sandstone was laid down in layers during the Permian and Triassic periods – anything up to 200 million years ago. The layers made it a relatively easy stone for the quarrymen to extract. Its colour can range from white to yellow, and red to brown. You will see plenty of white to grey sandstone in local buildings and much of this will have been quarried locally. There is also a great deal of red sandstone, and this is most likely to have been extracted from Woolton or Runcorn. The latter is largely confined to later work built after the arrival of rail transport. The creation of a rail network meant that stone could be moved cheaply from more distant quarries. This included various forms of granite, marble and high-quality limestone such as Portland stone. As all the local quarries have closed, the nearest source of red sandstone is (coincidentally) a quarry at Crosby Ravensworth in Cumbria.

The local sandstone can be seen as a natural outcrop in Little Crosby just under Little Crosby Hall's boundary wall near the large cross set by the villagers as a memorial to Squire Francis Nicholas Blundell in 1936. This sandstone was quarried close by on the west side of Delph Lane between Dibb Lane and Ackers Lane. Delph is a Lancashire word for a quarry or mine. According to Frank Tyrer's guide to Little Crosby, it was opened up sometime between 1610 and 1663. The 1850 large-scale Ordnance Survey map shows that it had grown into a large oblong hole measuring roughly 400 by 250 feet. It continued to be worked until 1890 when it was known as the Crane Pit. So much stone had been extracted that a crane was needed to lift out the stone. The reason for its closure is unclear. It could have been rendered unprofitable, or perhaps the beds of usable stone had been exhausted. It was probably the former because enormous of quantities of cheap but high-quality bricks were being brought in from North Wales and Accrington. The fact that some stone was later quarried to make F.N. Blundell's memorial points to the same conclusion. A postcard dated 1909 in Tom Heath's second book of Crosby pictures shows that the quarry had been flooded. In 1953 it was finally filled in.

The 1850 map also shows a Quarry House on the corner of Virgins Lane and Brook Road in Thornton, but no quarry. It was either too small to be marked or it had been filled in by the time of the survey. The present Quarry Road, which is the extension of Moor Lane in place of the original Ince Road, recalls this quarry. There were also quarries at Maghull (close to Westway), Melling (below the Bootle Arms) and Great Altcar (at New Hill House). The first two have been filled in while the latter is still extant though un-worked.

A sandstone outcrop can be seen in Little Crosby under the boundary wall of Little Crosby Hall alongside the memorial to F.N. Blundell.

The evidence of how much stone was extracted over the centuries is all around us in buildings, boundary walls and stone-paved tracks. The quarryman's techniques were essentially simple and unchanging. It was not a case of blowing up sections of the rock face. That would have only resulted in small unusable pieces. The main method was to prise the stone from its bed by drilling holes at intervals along a clearly visible natural splitting line. Plugs and feathers were inserted into these holes. The plug was a wedge-shaped iron rod and the feathers were two half-round sections of steel, which were inserted on either side of the plug. The plugs were then hammered down between the feathers causing the rock to split along the natural line. Once extracted, large blocks could be sawn or split into smaller building-size blocks. They could be further shaped using a variety of chisels and drags, which were worked with a specially shaped mason's mallet. Drags were steel combs, which could smooth or give a texture to the stone.

The detailed fine carving of the stone to fashion buildings, monuments and headstones was carried out by master or free masons, as opposed to the 'rough masons' working in the quarry. In Nicholas Blundell's time rough masons were known as 'stone-getters' and paid seven pence a day. Master masons received an extra two pence together with their food and drink. Mannex's Lancashire directory of 1854 lists a John Tomkinson as a stone merchant of Little Crosby. This suggests that the Blundells had let out the quarry on a commercial basis. You can see a good selection of mason's tools in the Village Museum, Little Crosby. Banners, an old Crosby firm of monumental masons, have their workshops nearby. The firm was founded by Hugh Banner in 1867 and had its original workshop more or less

The Norman capitals found at Sefton church are the oldest surviving carved stones in the Crosby area and Merchant Taylors' School is the oldest surviving secular stone building. Both Sefton church and the school have been defaced by schoolboy graffiti from the eighteenth and nineteenth centuries. These examples were drawn from the north wall of the school.

on the site of Bennett's glove factory on Mersey Road. It later moved to the corner of Coronation Road and Islington, and was compulsorily purchased to make way for the village by-pass in 1972. This is pictured on page 42 of Tom Heath's first book of Crosby photographs and shows a wide selection of headstones.

The earliest carved stones in the district are displayed in the Molyneux chapel of St Helen's church, Sefton. They are fragments of Norman capitals from the first church and have been dated to about 1170. The earliest complete stone building is the Merchant Taylors' original school building, which is part of the girls' school today. Opened for lessons in 1622, it was built along the lines of a Lancashire yeomans' house of the period with two storeys and a projecting porch. The ground floor was originally one large classroom with the headmaster teaching the seniors at one end and his assistant, the usher, the juniors at the other. The upper floor accommodated the usher and the school servants and the headmaster's house was to the east. John Harrison, the rich London merchant whose family had originated from Great Crosby, had drawn up plans for the endowment of the school in his lifetime and entrusted the implementation to a younger relative, also John Harrison. By the time of his death in 1619, a plot of land had been bought and building had started. John Harrison of Great Crosby turned out to be a lax administrator and the company had to take him to task for delays in the construction and failing to supervise John Turner, the freemason, properly. In June 1621, the clerk of the company in London received a letter from Harrison stating that 'he was very like to taste of a dish of hard dealing at the hand of John Turner, in the measuring [of] the work.' It appeared that Turner had cut down on the stonework by enlarging the size of the windows. Trouble with builders is clearly not a new phenomenon. Harrison let his accounts get into such a state that he and William Hunt of Sefton, the quarryman (or 'stone gatherer' as the accounts put it), were summoned to London to explain themselves. Today the building serves as a school library, and some of the older features remain such as one of the large blocked-in fireplaces in the classroom. The room over the entrance is known as the 'birching room' because tradition has it that the headmaster punished the boys there. Outside, there is a large amount of graffiti carved on the stones by nineteenth-century pupils – a rather more permanent inscription than sprayed paint.

The Blundells used stone not only for their own hall but also for the farm houses, stables, cowsheds and barns for their tenants because it was freely available on their land. As a result, Little Crosby has a wealth of stone buildings today. One group of cottages have a date stone of 1669. Further on there is a splendid series of barns. The stone for St Mary's church, which was built between 1845 and 1847, also came from the nearby quarry. It seems to have been planned on a similar scale and style (complete with a spire) to St Helen's, Sefton. The Blundells had their own pew at Sefton and many were buried there. But their brave adherence to the Catholic faith ruled them out of participating in the worship at St Helen's. There are more fine stone farm buildings at Crosby Hall Educational Trust, just off Back Lane. These are the old Home Farm buildings. The Great Barn, which is used for exhibitions and concerts, is believed to date back to the sixteenth century, and others in the complex are believed to date back to the seventeenth century.

Stone symbolises permanence and prestige and was employed in the building of many of the local churches. St Luke's parish church was the first of the new churches. It too was built with an impressive spire. Its building stone was quarried at Stourton (later Storeton) Hill on the Wirral, which was one of the biggest quarries on Merseyside. Its high quality Keuper sandstone was used to build many important local buildings such as the Liverpool Customs House (1828) and Birkenhead Town Hall (1883). Christ Church, Waterloo, (1894), is a massive red sandstone structure with a mighty north tower, which stands out as a landmark from the sea. Red sandstone from Runcorn was used for the United Reformed Church in Eshe Road North. Many church interiors were graced with stone as part of their structure and decoration. The interior of St Peter and Paul's church (1894), which has a mixture of Classical columns with Corinthian capitals and pointed Gothic arches, is one of the best local examples. The reredos is a beautiful confection of delicately carved stone tracery forming niches for statues and painted panels.

Sometimes public buildings and banks were built from stone as a mark as their status. In the case of banks it was symbolic of their stability and credit-worthiness. Waterloo Town Hall (now Crosby Town Hall) in Great Georges Road, Waterloo, was built of what appears to be local stone in 1862, with a taller extension at the back also constructed in stone in 1893. Although there are no banks built entirely of stone locally, some of them have impressive features in stone. The Westminster Bank (now the Old Bank pub) on South Road has a nice mixture of a red sandstone and mock-Tudor half-timbering. Lloyd's TSB, also on South Road, has a corner entrance with a huge shield carved with its rearing horse badge of Portland stone. This is the finest of white limestones and has tiny fossils in its texture.

Potter's Barn on Crosby Road South, Seaforth, is a red sandstone relic of a mansion building project. In 1841 it was to be the entrance and stables to a large house to be built

Above: The beautiful interior of the church of St Peter and St Paul, Liverpool Road, with its mixture of stone Corinthian columns and Gothic arches, which lead the eye to the three lancet windows and the wonderfully carved reredos below.

Left: Stonehouse: the marine engineer David Rollo's house in Waterloo Park is entirely faced in stone, unlike many other prestigious local villas of the same era.

for William Potter, a rich Liverpool merchant. It was modelled on the famous farm La Haye Saint, a pivotal place in the British line at the Battle of Waterloo in 1815. Potter's business failed and he ran out of the money to finish his dream. His red sandstone Barn remains as his memorial though sadly in a derelict condition. Seaforth Hall, which stood roughly where the Seaforth grain mills stand today, was the most elegant stone house in the area. A neo-Classical design by Sir James Picton, it was started in 1839. Its owner, James Muspratt, had made his fortune by pioneering a new way of making alkali, which was in huge demand in the textile and glass industries. His house with its elegant pediment and pillars facing the river was his way of celebrating his wealth and status. It was demolished in 1924 to make way for dock developments. Not a stone remains; only a fine photograph in the *Seaforth in Camera* book.

Stonehouse on Park Road is a magnificent three-storey villa (now turned into flats) in Waterloo Park. It looks as if it has been cleaned recently which brings out the golden yellow of the sandstone. It was built for the Rollo family about 1871. David Rollo was a Scottish engineer who built up a large marine engineering business in Liverpool and Birkenhead. It has touches of both Gothic and Italianate. By contrast, the front of 46 Kimberley Drive owes much to the kind of older rugged stone houses found in the Pennines with its narrow mullioned windows. It makes a nice contrast with its mock-Tudor neighbours. The Royal Oak Hotel, Warrenhouse Road, has a bit of both. It is mainly built of yellow sandstone combined with mock-Tudor timbers and a striking piece of Art Nouveau plasterwork in the main gable.

Use of stone for ornament and in combination with brick was a feature of many late nineteenth-century houses in Great Crosby and Waterloo. Some were built with a stone frontage with side and back walls built of brick. For example, you can see houses with stone fronts for the wealthier end of the market in Cambridge Road, Crosby Road North and Great Georges Road, Waterloo. Number 11 St Michael's Road at first glance seems to be a genuine late sixteenth-century house with the flagstone roof and the porch with its little obelisk surmounted by a ball, sturdy oak door and coat of arms. But it is dated 1913 and the two gables, which are partly camouflaged by climbing plants, are built of a dark rustic brick.

Many other local houses have stone incorporated into their structure. Window sills, jambs and lintels were often still made of stone in houses that were otherwise built of brick. Some of the lintels are decorated with carved work. Moorlands, Moor Lane and 12 to 14 Witham Avenue have particularly nice examples of trailing foliage. On some houses, such as those built by the Sawyer family in Victoria Road, Eshe Road and Liverpool Road, the window and door jambs have been given capitals of red sandstone carved into the shape of upright leaves. The keystones of the front doors in Rossett Road all have distinctive heads of kings and queens. In most late nineteenth-century houses these components are quite plain. But string courses of stone between bands of brick can be used to decorative effect. This was one of the features of Norman Shaw's work, and can be seen on a large scale on the White Star Line offices in James Street, Liverpool. It can also be seen in a much diluted form in local late nineteenth-century buildings such as the former bank in Bridge Road on the corner of Harlech Road. Stone was used in small quantities in some homes of the 1920s. A group of semi-detached houses on Liverpool Road and Dorbett Road have massive stone lintels to form their main entrances. In the 1960s there was a fashion for large stone-clad chimneys for bungalows, and local examples can be found on Esplen Avenue and Hall Road East.

Above: Number 11 St Michael's Road was built in 1913 and not in the sixteenth century, as might appear. Its two wings are built in rustic brick while the centre porch in white sandstone appears to be authentic Tudor. The roof is also covered with sandstone flags.

Left: Banks built prestigious buildings and none more so that Parr's Bank, later the Westminster Bank on South Road. It has a combination of red sandstone lower floors topped by elaborate timber-framed gable. The upper part of the bank was the manager's residence. Notice the side wall is built in brick which shows that even banks could not afford an all-stone building.

Above: Further up South Road, Lloyds Bank made its presence felt with a bold corner entrance topped by a large piece of sculpture in Portland stone.

Right: Many other houses have stone lintels and window sills. Some have carvings such as the houses of Rossett Road, which have different carved heads of kings or queens.

Many homes have their boundaries marked by stone gateposts. The variety of their styles is a study in its own right. Bottom left: a simple incised flower from Rossett Road. Bottom right: a Gothic style almost like a miniature shrine with inset trefoils – a symbol of the Trinity – from Stonehouse. Top right is from Kingsway and carries the name of the house. Top left: Alpha Lodge added to Rossett Road about 1900. Here the stone lintels and window framing along with the gateposts were in 'modern' orange moulded terracotta brick probably by Dennis & Co. of Ruabon.

Before all roads were covered in asphalt, stone setts were a common local road surface. You can find occasional traces of this surface on entrances to the backs of houses and businesses. This very good example leads off Coronation Road. Notice how long slabs have been used to smooth the passage of wheeled vehicles and the amount of wear from passing cart wheels on the setts inside these slabs.

'An Englishman's home is his castle' is an old cliché, but all around us you can see how much we value our privacy. One way this is expressed locally is in the boundary walls and gateposts in front of our houses. Most terraced houses do not have their front doors directly opening on to the street. They have a small strip of garden, a wall and a gate. The gate is often hung between two massive stone posts. These posts are usually finished off in a simple decorative form with a huge variety of shapes. Sometimes, the number or the name will be carved or painted on to these posts. Gateposts are also clues to where old Victorian houses used to be. Over the years many have been demolished and replaced by flats or groups of smaller houses, and quite often the stone gateposts and walls have been left. Forton Lodge on Blundellsands Road East and Leeswood on Park Road are two examples. The biggest boundary wall of all is the stone wall surrounding the park of Little Crosby Hall which was started in 1813. You will also find stones used as boundary markers between the different parishes. The Little Crosby-Great Crosby boundary stone is on Little Crosby Road opposite Boundary Cottage.

Unless it was thatch, the roof covering for local houses was almost always stone until the early twentieth century. Stone flagstones brought in from the Pennines were once used locally. The former Orchard farmhouse off Alexandra Road, the houses of Springfield

A Cumbrian Slate roof tops a pebble-dashed house with a splendid turret at the corner of Liverpool Road and Kingsway, the boudary of Great Crosby and Waterloo.

Terrace in Victoria Road and the original Merchant Taylors' building are the surviving examples. Welsh slate ranging from black to purple became the almost universal roofing material by the middle of the nineteenth century. Green Westmorland slate is less common, but can be found on local buildings ranging from the Birkey Hotel to Nazareth House and 'Blundellsands Hall' on the Serpentine. The green slates of the United Reformed Church in Eshe Road came from the Tilberthwaite Green quarry. Cumbrian Slate is a metamorphic rock, a substance that has been transformed by huge pressure and/or heat. It can be split into thin pieces. Millions of tons were quarried and exported all over England and Europe. You can still appreciate the huge scale of the workings by visiting the Welsh Slate Museum at Llanberis. Slate was also in Victorian pantries where a large slate slab would help keep perishable food cool.

Stone was also used for pavements, yards and some local roads. Sometimes it was in the form of squared blocks known as setts. The passages leading to garages and stores off Coronation Road are good examples of such road paving and they have the wear marks of the horse-drawn carts which once used them. Local farms also used slabs of stone for pig sties and fencing, and some can be seen near the Mill House just by Sefton church.

EIGHT
Bricks

Most buildings in Crosby are built of brick and are less than 150 years old. Yet brick making has a long history locally for, in spite of much of the land surface being sandy, there are good deposits of clay below. Clay is technically a rock, but it does not have the hard properties of stone. Instead it is plastic and adhesive; it can be watertight and with heat it can be baked hard. The earliest brick makers moulded the clay and left the resulting bricks to dry in the sun. This is impossible in the English climate and bricks have to be fired to harden them. There are many different types of clay. Fine white china clay found in Cornwall is used for making china wares; fire clay, found close to coal seams, makes good heat-resistant bricks for blast furnaces and railway fireboxes; and brick earth is more or less anything found near the surface and is often mixed with stones. Clay may contain various oxides, which will make the bricks different colours when they are fired: hence you find a huge variation in colour according to the origin of the clay.

The process of making bricks is basically the same whether they are made in a rural 'summer yard' or in a mechanised factory. The clay has to be extracted and then made plastic so that it can be moulded into bricks. The 'green' bricks have to be allowed to dry before they are finally fired hard. In the old rural way, clay was dug in the autumn and winter and left to 'weather'. In the following spring or summer it was ground in a large pan using a heavy upright millstone dragged round by a horse – a pug mill. The pugged clay was carried to the brick moulder, who would sprinkle sand into the wooden mould to ensure the clay did not stick and then throw in the required amount of clay and scrape off any surplus. The moulded green bricks would be carried away to dry. In a 'summer yard', they would be left in the open under a temporary shelter. Once they were judged to be dry enough they were stacked into a pyramid shape with coal dust or slack between them. They were covered with old bricks which were sealed with clay or turf. Tunnels were left in the base in which wood and coal were placed and set on fire. The clamp, as it was known, was allowed to burn itself out, resulting in bricks that were often varied in colour because of the different temperatures within.

Brick making became increasingly a big factory mechanised process in the nineteenth century. Steam engines could be used to power pug mills, stone removers, and moulding machines. Drying sheds using the waste heat from firing and patent Hoffman kilns (1858) made it possible to make bricks all the year round. The abolition of the Brick Tax in 1850 and the rapidly increasing demand as towns and factories expanded contributed to a rapid increase in production.

Most local bricks were of a pale reddish to buff colour, sometimes with touches of purple. I have found only one example of a stamped Crosby-made brick and that was among the piles of bricks on the shore between the Hall Road and Fort Crosby. It was of a deep orange-red, which suggests that the Moor Hey clay deposit was a purer clay than the normal local quality of clay.

Joseph Sawyer, who built Claremont Terrace in Victoria Road opposite the Duck Pond in the early 1870s, probably completed the houses with the same kinds of decorative brick elsewhere in Great Crosby. They can be seen in Liverpool Road, College Road and Eshe Road. They all have a moulded brick cornice with bands in two colours below them, and the same two-colour detailing around the bays and the front door, so it is probable that were all built by the same builder.

Local brick making is believed to have started at the beginning of the seventeenth century. An early reference can be found in the will of William Abraham of Thornton, which included a stock of bricks valued at three shillings and four pence. Of course, there is no way of telling whether or not they were made locally. However, given the condition of the roads, the chances are that they were. In 1692 the Halmote records for Great Crosby refer to John Chorley's tenancy of fields called Brickfield Hey, measuring about an acre. The Tithe Map of 1844 recorded four fields named Brick Kiln at the junction of Moor Lane and Forefield Lane and another in what became Waterloo Park as Brick or High Field. There was also another close to centre of Great Crosby, which is commemorated in Kilnyard Road at the back of Coronation Road. All these field names must refer to where clay had been dug and bricks fired. In other words, it was intermittent production, carried out as and when needed.

Nicholas Blundell recorded his own brick making. In January 1719, he brought in an itinerant master brick maker. The first step was to use an auger to bore down to find the right kind of clay. Then this was dug out and left to weather. He had a sample of the clay tested at a pottery ('the Mugg House and Pipe Works') in Liverpool. The test was satisfactory, but the clay was left until 17 June, and the moulding and drying took until the end of August. The firing of the two clamps, which were sealed with turf, took a week. The coal slack came from the nearest mines at Prescot and was transported in his own cart using the labour of some of his tenants who owed him boon work. In all, 200,000 bricks were produced. Many of these were used to build a house and chapel for Father Aldred, his chaplain, and this is presumably the Priest's House, which still stands in Little Crosby today.

Local brick making must have continued on a similar basis until the mid-nineteenth century. As already mentioned in chapter three, there are a number of brick-built houses in the district that have survived from the late eighteenth century or early nineteenth century. These must have been built with local bricks. There were no brick works marked on the 1850 Ordnance Survey map. However the local directories list a number of works from 1871. In that year William Humphreys was listed as a brick maker in Victoria Road. His clay pit was probably at the junction of Victoria Road and Cooks Road where there is still a distinct dip in the ground behind the houses fronting Cooks Road. There was the Moor Hey Brick & Tile Co., the Crosby Brickworks, Moor Lane, and the Crosby Terra-Cotta Ornamental Brick & Tile Works in Forefield Lane listed in the local directories in 1881, 1886 and 1891. It is likely these were the same works under different names. The 1891 Ordnance Survey map shows that there were some substantial buildings on the south side of Forefield Lane. By 1894, it was presumably closed because it was no longer listed in the directories. The 1907 Ordnance Survey map showed an old clay pit in one of the fields to the north of Forefield Lane. You can still find the occasional Moor Hey brick on the sea defences between Hall Road and Hightown. There was also a brick works owned by Brooks & Whitehouse on College Road. In July 1902, the local council took them to court for causing a nuisance by the emission of large quantities of dense black smoke from their clamps. The most likely site is in what were fields between Brooke Road East and Victoria Park where a large pit is marked on the 1907 map. Today, this area is covered by the 'dale' roads – Ferndale, Oakdale, Thorndale – all homes built in the 1920s or '30s.

The biggest local works was on Cooks Road. This seems to have started in about 1892 and the *Crosby Herald* paid a visit there in 1898. Their reporter were guided round by the manager, Mr Edward Peters, who told him that it was the only brick works between Bootle and Southport that made bricks by machine. There were forty workmen and at the time they were engaged digging clay some fifteen to twenty feet below the surface. The clay

Left: The 'diaper pattern' of diamonds outlined in a different colour of brick can be found on these small terraced houses on Victoria Road and on more prestigious dwellings such as the Sacred Heart School.

Below: Numbers 42 and 44 Myers Road West have an unusual patterning. The stretchers and the headers are in different coloured brick and there are three colours of brick around the upper windows and the front door.

was shovelled into narrow-gauge railway wagons, which were drawn up by a steam winch to a platform where they were automatically tipped into a hopper. From there the clay fell into the grinding machine and moved on to the pugging machine. It was then extruded in a brick-shaped 'sausage' and cut into brick-sized pieces by a cutting machine. The bricks were carried to the drying house, which was capable of drying up to 55,000 bricks at a time. They spent four days there being gently dried. Tiers of brick were built up and fires lit at each end of the kiln. Between 25,000 and 30,000 bricks could be produced every day. These were common wire-cut bricks as opposed to the better-quality pressed brick. The works was having difficulty keeping up with its orders during this local building boom. A cottage consumed 30,000 bricks while a villa in Blundellsands needed about 150,000. The 1907 Ordnance Survey map shows a large pit about 500 by 300 feet, demonstrating how much clay had been extracted. By 1915, it was known as the Great Crosby Machine Brick Co. Ltd and it seems to have closed around 1921. The site of the clay pit is now the playing field of Valewood School. There were other brick works operating at Hightown and Seaforth in the early twentieth century. The site of the former was in the area of St Stephen's Way and Hester Close, while the latter lies under the Seaforth Dock complex.

The role of the Sawyer family is one of the mysteries of local brick making. In 1856, a Joseph Sawyer, bricklayer of Waterloo, bought a portion of the Holme Field between Cooks Road and Little Crosby Road. He may have built Lupton Cottages there (as shown on the 1907 map) or perhaps he found clay there and made bricks. In 1871, John, Joseph and Richard Sawyer were listed as bricklayers living in Waterloo. In that year, they also built Claremont Terrace (18-26) Victoria Road West. The bricks for number 26 (at least) were stamped 'Sawyer' and yet they were never listed as brick makers. It is unusual in my experience for anyone except the brick maker to put his name on bricks. On the other hand, they built a large number of houses locally, many of which they rented out.

Local brick makers in all parts of the country had to compete with mass-produced bricks brought in by the railways. Bricks from outside the district are much in evidence in local buildings dating from the last quarter of the nineteenth century. You can tell because most of the outside products are a distinctive orange-red. They came from two main areas: North Lancashire, centred around Accrington, and North Wales, centred around Ruabon. They were both coal mining areas with rich seams of fire clay, which made fine bricks. These were much stronger and smoother than the standard Crosby product and were good at resisting attack from salt air and industrial pollution. As a result, 'Ruabon Reds' and 'Accrington Bloods' can be found all over the North West in cotton mills and other factories, seaside resorts such as Southport and Blackpool, churches and chapels and in thousands of houses. They were similar in colour and it is impossible to tell them apart unless you can see the maker's name stamped in the frog of the brick. Incidentally, you can see lots of examples of the different maker's names among the bricks and tiles that have been tipped on the beach between the coastguard station, Hall Road and Hightown.

The scale of the works was huge and at their peak before the First World War provided work for thousands of men and boys. The main period of growth started in the 1880s. In the Accrington area the major works included the Accrington Brick & Tile Co. established in 1887 (on the site of a smaller works), the Altham Brick & Tile Co. of 1890, the Whinney Hill Brick & Tile Co. about 1890 and the Huncoat Brick & Tile Co. of 1894. Examples of their products can be found in our area. The most common seems to be those of the Altham works which had the brand name Nori, i.e. iron backwards. Such was the scale of industry that Whittakers, an Accrington firm of engineers, began making their own patent brick presses in 1894.

Left: This terrace opposite the Duck Pond in Cambridge Road, Great Crosby, has unusual chamfers to the upper floor of its bay. This feature can also been found on other local terraces such as those on Cambridge Road, Waterloo and Cooks Road. Perhaps they were all built by the same builder?

Below: Council houses built by Sefton Rural District Council in Runnells Lane in 1926.

Other types of brick became popular in the 1930s such as these cream-coloured blocks with black edgings and lettering. Cremona Corner looks almost like the bows of a ship with the three stripes on either side of the name.

While the Accrington works seem to have concentrated mainly on bricks and tiles, the brick works of North Wales had a much wider range of products. The scale of the North Wales brick-making industry is demonstrated in Andrew Connolly's book *Life in the Victorian Brickyards of Flintshire and Denbighshire*. It contains a list of 127 brick works between Ruabon in the south and Connah's Quay in the north. Those around Ruabon and Wrexham mainly produced the hard red bricks so popular in Crosby. Among the many firms, Monk & Newell, who were Liverpool building contractors, established a new works at Ruabon in 1883 and took a full-page advertisement in the Gore's Liverpool Directories. This included a view of the works with its 174-foot chimney, steam-heated drying sheds and circular kilns. Their products included bricks in red, blue, brindled and buff, pressed or wire-cut, moulded bricks with decoration such as dentil, dogtooth and diaper, copings for gables, roofing tiles, tiles for hanging on outside walls, floor tiles and decorative terra cotta. They employed a full-time modeller, a Mr H.M. Whyte of London, to produce the designs for the ornamental work, and these were made into dies into which clay was pressed by a battery of brick presses. The fineness of the clay also meant that it could be moulded into intricate patterns for tiles, plaques, finials and all manner of architectural detailing. The Alfred Palmer Centre for Archives and Local History at Wrexham Museum has catalogues from some of the local brick works: J.C. Edwards & Co. dating from 1883, the Ruabon Brick & Tile Co. from about 1901 and Dennis & Co. from 1929. These show the wonderful selection of decorative building materials on offer. The

A tour-de-force in Ruabon brick, a Classical entrance with shell motif to be seen on houses between numbers 30 and 38 Oxford Road.

Edwards' catalogue starts with a set of illustrations of major commissions which included the Liverpool Training College. This was designed by T. Mellarde Read (junior), the Blundellsands architect, and he certainly used this type of brick in the houses he built locally.

There are many late nineteenth-century and early twentieth-century decorative brick panels, ridge tiles, chimney pots and finials on houses and shops around Crosby and Waterloo today. It is impossible to determine where most of them were made. It is possible that some in buildings put up before 1894 were made locally by the Crosby Terra-Cotta Ornamental Brick & Tile Co. The large terraced and semi-detached houses that the Sawyers built in the 1870s on Victoria Road, Eshe Road, College Road and Liverpool Road all have decorative brick cornices just below the eaves. It is possible that this ornament was locally produced. They also have decorative bands of bricks in two colours below the cornice and around the bays and front door. Another variation on this was to use two colours of brick in the main part of the wall either alternating, as you can see on some of the houses on the south side of Waterloo Road, or as a diaper (diamond) pattern. This can be seen, for example, in the small terraces of Victoria Road, Great Crosby and in the main building of the Sacred Heart School.

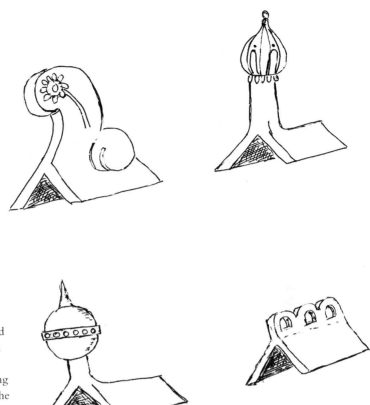

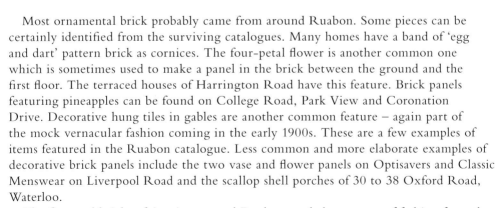

A medley of finials and ridge tiles drawn from around Coronation Road and neighbouring streets. All appear in the Ruabon Brick & Terra-Cotta Co.'s catalogues.

Most ornamental brick probably came from around Ruabon. Some pieces can be certainly identified from the surviving catalogues. Many homes have a band of 'egg and dart' pattern brick as cornices. The four-petal flower is another common one which is sometimes used to make a panel in the brick between the ground and the first floor. The terraced houses of Harrington Road have this feature. Brick panels featuring pineapples can be found on College Road, Park View and Coronation Drive. Decorative hung tiles in gables are another common feature – again part of the mock vernacular fashion coming in the early 1900s. These are a few examples of items featured in the Ruabon catalogue. Less common and more elaborate examples of decorative brick panels include the two vase and flower panels on Optisavers and Classic Menswear on Liverpool Road and the scallop shell porches of 30 to 38 Oxford Road, Waterloo.

The fiery red bricks of Accrington and Ruabon tended to go out of fashion from the 1920s. Other kinds of less colourful brick were preferred. For example, the six early council houses erected by Sefton Rural District Council in 1926 in Runnel's Lane, along with similar ones on Edge Lane and Ince Road, Thornton, were built in a darker type of brick. Many houses of that decade were part or wholly covered in pebble-dash.

A selection of ornamental bricks. From left to right and top to bottom: vase with foliage and flowers on first floor of Optisavers (formerly Irwins, the grocers); pedimented panel with flower and leaves and scroll, 44 Liverpool Road; rustic brick in diamond pattern with blue brick borders, MacDonald's newsagents and adjacent shops, College Road; 'daisy' and 'rose' in College Road North; pineapple and flower surrounded by small flowers, Myers Road East, College Road and other adjacent roads; 'egg and dart' cornice with a band of small flowers below in Oxford Road and many other roads.

A fine set of salt-glazed chimney pots in Kimberley Drive, with the small flat tiles favoured in the mock vernacular style of the early twentieth century.

Rustic bricks became increasingly popular. This meant that the surface was roughened as if it had been produced in a rural brick works and the Dennis Catalogue for 1929 included examples of rustic bricks alongside the fiery red ones. You can see several examples of this type of brick inlaid in patterns in the parapets hiding the slate roofs of the single-storey shops of the 1920s, for example on College Road starting with MacDonald's, the newsagent or in the ground-floor panels of the Alexandra in South Road.

Some of the shops of the next decade are more striking because they are built with cream polished facing bricks. The ones on the south side of Moor Lane in Crosby Village are dated 1936. There are similar ones on the south side of Endbutt Lane at its junction with Liverpool Road, a pair of shops (one the former post office) on Brownmoor Lane and at the junction of South Road and Crosby Road North. The latter are named Cremona Corner after the large house to which they have been added. This was once a noted music school established in 1880 and Cremona in Italy was the home town of all the best violin makers. It is impossible to tell where modern brick comes from, but it is noticeable that many post-Second World War houses are built in various shades of buff and brown brick rather than the reds preferred by earlier generations of local builders.

NINE

Concrete, Glass, Steel, Cast Iron and other Metallic Substances

Concrete or cement is the later version of mortar – a substance for bonding together bricks and stones to make a building. Concrete can be a structural member or the covering of a building as well. There is a great deal of concrete in its various forms around our district. Mortar is made by mixing roasted lime (quick lime) with water and sand. However it tends to be porous and not set as hard as concrete. In 1820, Portland cement was patented and this was a mixture of clay and lime roasted together, and when this was mixed with water and sand set much harder than mortar. It was called Portland because it was supposed to resemble Portland stone. The use of cement (concrete) took a major step with the development of reinforced concrete. Although there had been experiments with embedding steel rods in concrete as early as the 1840s to make things like beams and flower pots, the first important reinforced concrete building system was developed by a Frenchman, Francois Hennebique, in the 1890s. The fifteen-storey Liver Building, which opened in 1911 with a reinforced concrete frame clad in granite, was probably the first major building made with this material anywhere in the country.

Reinforced concrete became increasingly popular with the Modernist architects and developers. The Modernists wanted to shed all the unnecessary decoration that had cluttered up buildings in the past, and developers wanted larger buildings that could be built quickly and therefore more cheaply. After the Second World War, there was a chronic shortage of houses, especially in Waterloo and Seaforth and building blocks of flats was one of the ways of tackling the shortage. The local council had powers to clear slum properties from 1925 and had built 197 council houses by 1939. Between 1945 and 1974, when Crosby Council became part of Sefton, another 3,200 dwellings were added. Some of these were in three- or four-storey maisonettes, some were traditional houses and the rest were in five fifteen-storey towers – two in Waterloo and three in Seaforth. All the different types used reinforced concrete in their structure. The houses and maisonettes had reinforced concrete lintels and in some cases porches. The houses on the Woodend estate are good examples. The towers had not only reinforced concrete frames, but cladding panels which were cast in a factory. Reinforced concrete can also be seen in the major buildings in Waterloo along Crosby Road North, such as the library opened in 1968, and the Pioneer Life Assurance House which opened next to it in the early 1970s and is now used as an IT training centre. The original swimming baths built on Mariner's Road in 1963 were a major addition to local amenities, and were also built of reinforced concrete. Costains, the local builders who

Concrete and mock-Tudor: one of the two tower blocks in Waterloo fronted by the old offices of that great local institution, the *Crosby Herald*.

developed into a national firm, also manufactured reinforced concrete railway sleepers and you can see examples of their products (with their name cast into them) under the tracks of the Northern Line. The biggest local reinforced concrete buildings are the grain silos at Royal Seaforth Dock, which were opened in 1974, and of course the walls of the dock itself depend on reinforced concrete for their strength.

The widest use of concrete was to bond bricks in houses and as an outer covering. At first this was a smoothed surface covering a brick wall, known as stucco. This was originally lime and sand but cement was rapidly substituted in the early nineteenth century. It became fashionable in London where John Nash built fine terraces for the wealthy to rent. These were built with inferior bricks, which were covered with a thick coating of stucco to render them weatherproof and to provide a stone-like finish which could be finished off with a coat of paint. Ornaments such as the tops of capitals could also be cheaply moulded rather than carved from stone. The original seaside terraces of Waterloo are treated with stucco to give a graceful appearance and to protect their brickwork from damage by the salt-laden air. Other isolated early nineteenth-century gentlemen's houses in Crosby were also built with stucco.

A fine example of pargeting with curving leafy forms around a central plaque can be seen in the gable of the Royal Oak, Warrenhouse Road.

The stucco fashion passed and most houses were built of plain brick until the late 1890s when a new fashion for cement rendering arrived in the district. This became known as rough casting or pebble-dash. It was used as far back as Tudor times and was an outer layer of lime plaster mixed with small stones. It was popular in Scotland where it was known as harling. It was another element borrowed from old vernacular buildings by some of the late Victorian or Edwardian architects. In their version a final layer (usually cement) was left to go sufficiently sticky to allow pea-sized gravel to be thrown on to it – hence pebble-dash. You can see a lot of different ways of using pebble-dash around the district. Some houses are entirely covered in it. Others have a brick ground floor and a pebble-dashed upper storey as well as mock-Tudor timbering. Some are painted and others not. Blundellsands and Hightown are notable for the large number of houses with white-painted pebble-dashed walls. Pebble-dash has also been applied to houses which were built without it and while this may be a way of protecting the brickwork it can be unsightly, especially if the pebble-dashed house is part of a terrace.

Pargeting was another form of decorative plaster decoration for half-timbered houses in the sixteenth and seventeenth centuries, especially in Essex and Suffolk. It was revived for Edwardian houses and there are a few local examples, which are all more or less to the same pattern. These include the Royal Oak Hotel, Exchange Buildings in Crosby Village and numbers 12, 29, 26, 28 and 35 Kimberley Drive. All of them have gables with different plasterwork patterns in relief with sinuous acanthus leaves and sometimes a shield or cartouche as a centrepiece. Numbers 64 and 66 Coronation Drive have a variation where

There is plenty of fine stained glass in local churches. Lesser examples can also be seen in local pubs such as the George, which has these fake heraldic devices in the upper lights of its main windows.

the plasterwork is in the bay windows between the ground and the first floor and is incised rather than in relief. Plastering, whether it is internal or external, is a real skill and yet only requires simple tools. There is a good set donated by Blanchards of Myers Road West in the Village Museum, Little Crosby. Occasionally you will also see decorative concrete panels. The most notable of these are the row of Viking ships on the front of the Plaza cinema. The classrooms of St Mary's College which back on to Claremont Road have a series of concrete panels depicting an angel holding a book with the Greek letters alpha and omega – the beginning and the end – inspired by the last book of the New Testament, the Book of Revelation.

Glass shares some of the ingredients of concrete because it is made by heating fine-quality sand and lime with soda as an additional ingredient. The resulting molten glass can be cast into sheets for windows or moulded into a whole range of domestic objects from milk bottles to wine glasses. Different chemicals can be added to the mix to produce a wide variety of colours. Window glass, which we take for granted, was a rare commodity except in churches and the homes of the gentry until the eighteenth century. It was also produced in small pieces and so it was common to mount small (usually diamond-shaped) pieces in strips of lead. Very little medieval glass has survived because churches were purged of popish ornaments by the Puritans of the Church of England after Henry VIII's Reformation. There are a few coloured fragments in St Helen's church, Sefton. The Gothic revival in the nineteenth century and the return to a more ritualistic way of worship saw the revival of stained glass in churches, and our local churches contain a great deal of coloured glass which was often donated in memory of members of local wealthy families. Some of the colours can be garish, but the best have the depth of colour of medieval glass. Possibly the best local windows are those by the Belgian artist Capronnier made between 1866 and 1877 in the transepts of St Luke's parish church which were donated by Richard Houghton in memory of three of his children. Stained glass had been a feature of Tudor and Jacobean houses and often consisted of armorial designs. There are some fifteenth-century good examples at Speke Hall. The revival of Tudor features for the great housing development of the 1900s include the re-introduction of leaded lights and stained glass. For most homes, the windows were framed in a Tudor style quite unlike the vertically orientated sash windows prevalent in Georgian and Victorian houses. The emphasis was horizontal with three or more lights often in a bay with a horizontal transom dividing the lights between a tall lower one with a small one above. The upper ones were often decorated with stained glass. Some of the grander local houses of the early 1900s also had large stained-glass windows lighting the stairs. The houses on Park Road, Waterloo have this arrangement. The fashion continued into the twenties and thirties, when many local houses were built with coloured glass windows in their front doors and in their front bay windows. Books on the architecture of these inter-war years often contain illustrations of stained-glass windows depicting galleons in full sail as typical for homes. So far, I have not come across any locally. Stained glass and leaded lights have never gone out of fashion for houses and you can see many recent examples in plastic double-glazed windows, and diamond lights can be bought as stick-on strips.

Iron is the most common metal used in the exterior of buildings and comes in various forms, such as wrought iron for gates and door fittings, cast iron for columns, gutters and down spouts, corrugated iron as a roofing material or mild steel for window frames. Wrought iron is made by smelting iron ore and then hammering it. It could be forged in ornamental shapes and you will find local examples such as the elaborate wrought-iron door hinges on the Threlfall mock-Tudor pubs. There are nice examples on one of the side doors of Merchant Taylors' School for Girls, which is in the shape of a Viking dragon, and on the doors of the old police station in Church Road, Waterloo. The former Blundellsands Hotel has a fine pair of wrought-iron gates, as does Bowersdale Park in Seaforth. The former drill hall of the 7th Battalion, the King's Regiment in Coronation Road (now the Crosby Youth Centre) has two large double doors which are decorated with large square-headed nails. They serve no functional purpose but are a reminder of the kind of defensive doors that once defended castles. Hand-cut wrought-iron nails were used for all kinds of fastening jobs before screws were available. The door leading from the upper floor of the old Merchant Taylors' School building is fastened in this way and this suggests that it might be part of the original fittings. They are a reminder that the blacksmith not only attended to shoeing horses, but was responsible for making all kinds of architectural fittings and mending agricultural implements. Modern wrought iron, which is usually mentioned in the same breath as gates, is no such thing. It is mild steel welded to make ornamental gates in the style of the wrought iron. There has been a recent fashion for these, especially the large automatically controlled variety, which are both decorative and a security barrier.

Cast iron is molten iron that has been poured into moulds. Wooden patterns of the object to be cast are made and then used to make the shape in special moulding sand. Cast iron became plentiful with the development of more productive iron-producing techniques in the eighteenth century. It was very good in compression but not in tension. This made it useful in buildings for making supporting columns, but was not good for beams that spanned unsupported spaces. The most common use was for gutters, rainwater heads and

Medieval-style wrought-iron door hinges at
Merchant Taylors' School for Girls (above
right) and the old police station, Church
Road, Waterloo (right).

One of the Art Nouveau wrought-iron gates of the former Blundellsands Hotel – all bulbous
swellings and curly tendrils.

While Marine Crescent and its neighbouring terraces are well known for their delicate cast-iron verandas, there are plenty of good, if lesser known, examples such as this elegant porch on Kingsway, Waterloo.

downspouts. You will see the occasional house with cast-iron columns, such numbers 4 to 8 York Road, which have barley-sugar twist columns as part of their window frames on the first floors. You can also find cast-iron columns in the windows of houses on Harbord Road, Waterloo, and number 1 Lulworth Road has a column supporting its corner to allow for a corner front door. Cast-iron gateposts can also be found, such as those at the entrance to St Mary's College. This was built as Claremont House for John Da Costa, a Liverpool merchant with American connections, and this is reflected in the eagle emblem of the United States cast into these gate posts.

Cast iron can be moulded into delicate and intricate shapes and the great glory of the local cast-iron architecture are the cast iron and glass verandas that front the seaside terraces of Waterloo. These graceful shelters with their frilly spandrels are the epitome of 'seaside architecture'. There are other elegant examples such as the arcade at Waterloo Hospital and the porches on houses on Kingsway that are the nearest to St Faith's church.

Cast iron is also a very durable material, which made it a useful material for street furniture. Lamp posts, pillar boxes, bollards, gateposts, railings, tram poles and telephone boxes, drainage grids and drain covers were among other many ordinary items that were made in cast iron. Most of the older local examples have been replaced.

Cast iron is a versatile material. Top right: cast-iron cannon protecting the boundary wall of St Luke's churchyard; top left, an elaborate bollard on Coronation Drive. Bottom left: a little heraldic lion on the railings of Forefield Lane School; right, cast-iron railing on the corner of Agnes Road and Blundellsands Road West.

The only Nissen hut left in the district? This deteriorating example of Second World War accommodation for military personnel is on Byrom Road at Hall's Vehicle Services depot.

The famous Five Lamps in Waterloo was originally an elaborately decorated single column that was displaced by the war memorial. The Waterloo Conservation Area appears to have its original lamp posts, but their slenderness and their height gives away the fact that they are modern steel replicas. Pillar boxes survive, but the traditional telephone box has disappeared except for one preserved example in the front garden of a house in Dorbett Road. Other cast-iron objects have been preserved as garden ornaments. There are at least two cast-iron mangles sitting brightly painted in front gardens in Crosby and Thornton.

Cast-iron bollards to bar vehicles from entering alleyways and to protect walls from damage are another type of cast-iron street furniture. There is a nice decorative one at the Liverpool end of Coronation Drive and numerous new ones to protect pavements from being parked on by vehicles. The most interesting one is the one that protects the southern boundary wall of St Luke's churchyard. It is on the forecourt of the Crosby Hotel and is a partially buried cast-iron muzzle-loading cannon. It seems a strange object to be found in Crosby. In fact, redundant cannon were used all round Liverpool as bollards. The Maritime Museum has one example. The Crosby example is a small calibre gun which fired a three-pound ball. It was probably one of the many guns carried by local merchant sailing ships in the early nineteenth century to protect themselves from pirate attacks. By 1853, when the wall was built, the Royal Navy exercised such tight control of the High Seas that piracy – except in the China Seas – was a thing of the past. There is a noticeable suite of cast-iron railings lining the approaches of the railway bridge on Mersey Road and the same pattern of railing is to be seen around the pedestrian underpass at Blundellsand station, and this

A clutch of pinnacles. Top right:
the domes of College Road Library
inspired by seventeenth-century
Baroque; top left: one of the Flying
Saucers of Crown Buildings.
Right: high Gothic spirelet at
St Nicholas, Blundellsands; and
above: outdoing every other local
pinnacle – the central tower of
Merchant Taylors' School for Boys.

Above and left: Cast-iron man wades out to sea mark – part of Anthony Gormley's installation on the beach, while another cast-iron man watches a passing ship.

suggests that these were all installed at the time of the building of the over bridge in the 1880s.

Cast iron can take on great detail and many components carry their maker's names, which can tell us a great deal about local manufacturers and their products. A humble grid in the alley between Ashlar Road and Fir Road was cast by the Brookfield Foundry, St Helen's. Cast iron was also good for decorative details. The defunct, battered drinking fountain with its supervising nymph in Alexandra Park is a good example. The latest manifestation of cast iron is on the beach. Anthony Gormley's sculpture 'Another Place' consists of 100 cast-iron statues moulded from his own body. It has caused great delight and great controversy.

Steel is an extremely tough malleable alloy of iron and carbon, which was used as a structural material for buildings from the early 1900s. Combined with glass it is very much on show in some of the new developments. The Mariner's Quay apartments which replaced a Victorian villa, the Knowles on Blundellsands Road West and Seapoint, a renovated villa nearby, both have huge glass and steel frontages. A humbler use of steel was the Nissen hut. This was a tunnel-shaped structure formed by bending sheets of corrugated iron (actually galvanized steel) to make the walls and roof one continuous element. It was named after Lt-Col. P.N. Nissen (1871-1950) who invented this and had it adopted as a cheap and quick way of providing accommodation for troops. There must have been many of these huts in the Second World War encampments around Crosby. Hall's Vehicle Services in Byrom Road still have a Nissen hut.

Steel was also used for window frames in 1930s houses. Crittalls of Braintree, Essex were the most notable producers. They were a different shape to the mock-Tudor ones with minimal glazing bars and an emphasis on the horizontal and often curved round a bay to maximise the light. Burbo Bank House is a good example – a block of flats overlooking the shore with semi-circular bays on each end which makes it look like the bridge of one of the great passenger liners of the 1930s. The 1930s shops in Moor Lane and Endbutt Lane have another variation with herringbone-shaped glazing bars.

Non-ferrous metals, especially lead and copper, make good if expensive roof coverings, and there are some distinctive examples on churches and public buildings. The 1960s fire station in Waterloo has a copper roof. St Faith's church has a low brick tower on its south side with a mini spire (fleche) clad in copper, as does the Methodist chapel on Moor Lane. St Nicholas, Bridge Road, has an impressive fleche in lead with decorative ribs. The pepper pot-shaped miniature domes of Jacobean mansions were another feature copied by late nineteenth-century architects. Among the local examples, we have two on College Road Library and a pair on each end of Crown Buildings, which look like flying saucers. Lead was the preferred covering for the upper works of the biggest tower in Crosby at Merchant Taylors' School for Boys, which resembles a younger brother of Big Ben.

TEN

Signs, Dates and Inscriptions

As you have seen from the previous chapters, you can find many aspects of Crosby's history and development through its buildings and their materials and through other material survivals, which range from objects to archives. You can also read the history of Crosby in the streets through signs, inscriptions and dates on buildings and in graveyards, and quite often they can throw a new light on the history of the district and lead us to discovering forgotten local characters or heroes.

Signs are all around us. On the streets, they tell us to stop, forbid us from parking, or turning, warn us of hazards ahead and generally exhort us to behave ourselves whether we are drivers, cyclists, pedestrians or dog owners. Then all the shops, pubs, bars and any other commercial outfit have signs advertising themselves. Many carry the logos of nationwide chains and are often so large they dominate their environment. Plastics, lighting and computer-aided design and cutting make them slick and eye-catching. Some attract with humour: 'Stamps' is a bar in the old Great Crosby Post Office and 'Curtains For You' which sells curtains and fabrics on Crosby Road North, Waterloo, made it into a compilation of the funniest shop signs across the whole of Britain.

It was not like that in the past. The photographs of the streets in the early twentieth century of Great Crosby and Waterloo show there were far fewer signs of all kinds. There could be some big ones such as the huge painted signboards on the old George and Brooke Hotels. Large individual gilded wooden letters advertised national brands such as Hovis Bread or individual establishments such as the Seaforth Arms which still has them. Most shops had painted signboards or white enamelled letters stuck on their windows or gilded lettering under glass panels. There were also enamelled metal advertisements for products such as Pratts' Motor Spirit or Mansion Polish. Gable ends were sometimes covered with large painted signs, and there were cast-iron street signs. Only those latter signs are with us today because of their durability. Enamelled signs advertising old brands are full of nostalgia and highly collectable, and there are some good examples in the Village Museum. You may spot the odd one still in situ, such as the Snowcem sign on the wall of a builder's yard in Brighton Road, Waterloo, and there are the remains of painted signs on brick walls, For example: 'James Powell, plumber', on the garden wall of 32 Bridge Road or 'R.D. Dewhurst, decorator', on the end of a wall of a derelict shop in Church Road, Waterloo and 'Gilbertson, the tarmac suppliers', in Cambridge Avenue, Crosby. There is the occasional old shop sign still in use: Satterthwaites have retained their 1930s lettering. Byron & Sons, which was started around 1940 in Coronation Road, has impeccable painted signs with shaded letters, and Cook's Stores in Oxford Road, Waterloo, has an old

Above: One of the few enamelled signs left, a Snowcem sign in a builder's yard on Brighton Road, Waterloo.

Right: The Westminster Bank sign on the former bank on College Road. The Old Bank in South Road still has a night safe in the wall with a Westminster Bank badge on it.

painted sign. The financial adviser's office on the corner of College Road and Brompton Avenue used to be a bank and still carries the Westminster Bank coat of arms and the Old Comrade's Club on Liverpool Road has a little carved roundel of St Luke high up in its gable which dates from the time when it was St Luke's parish hall. Before that it was the Bousefield family's home, The Hawthorns, and you can still see the gable of the old house poking above the modern frontage.

The names of local houses are an intriguing study. Going back to the rural past, there were so few dwellings that even modest homes and terraces invariably had a name. These usually reflected their position. Hence in 1850 there was Big Pit Farm on Out Lane (Victoria Road) or Stanfield Terrace on Liverpool Road. In the second half of the nineteenth century, the higher the status of the house, the more likely it was to have a name. In 1900, Blundellsands and Waterloo Park were distinguished from the rest of the district because they had names without numbers. By then, most of the names did not refer to the setting of the house but to places which meant something special to their owners. So, for a typical sample, on the right-hand side of Merrilocks Road there were Glynnhurst, Rearsby, Erstwood, Rosslyn, Rotherslade, Dalmore, Norrland, Lynton, Brocklehurst, Tacoma, Cintra, Ingerthorpe, The Withens, The Holt, Alexandra House, Inglenook and Kirriemuir. Most of these names are places outside the district. There were three Scottish place-names which reflected a wider popularity of Scottish names throughout the district. Some were places abroad such as Cintra and Tacoma. The Withens, The Holt and Inglenook all hinted at a domestic retreat. Only Parkfield was drawn from the house's location. The other exception was Lynton, which was owned by William Sproule who was a shipowner. The pride of his fleet was a 2,531-ton steel four-masted barque built by R. & J. Evans at Liverpool in 1894 and called the *Lynton*. She was noted for having a large number of sails and was very fast. He and his partners sold her to London owners in 1900. She was finally sunk by a German submarine whilst under the Russian flag in 1917. Lynton, the house, has been demolished, but the name continues for the block of flats that replaced it.

Incidentally, while on the subject of ships, two sailing ships, the *Waterloo* and the *Seaforth* of 1862 and 1863, were among the most advanced sailing ships of their time. There is a model of a sister ship, the *Evelyn*, in the Maritime Museum's collection. There were a number of ships called *Crosby*, including a cargo liner owned by the Gulf Line of London of 1907 and several tugs owned by the Alexandra Towing Co. of Liverpool.

There are a number of plaques and date stones (or moulded brick ones) on houses, shops and other buildings around the district. They range from 1813 to 2004. Many are hard to spot because they have been placed high up on buildings on rainwater heads. I am not sure I have spotted all of them. But those I have collected give a good idea of the development of the district. There are only six before 1850: 1813 is the date of the windmill erected by William Blundell, 1815 on a house in Bath Street, Waterloo, (though I suspect this is a later installation), 1826 with the initials KGE on a rainwater head on 155 Liverpool Road, 1841 on Potter's Barn, 1842 on the National School, Great Georges Road, Waterloo, and 1846 on numbers 6 and 8 Vale Road, Crosby. St Luke's Halsall School has a potted history on a plaque in the school playground which shows the school was first built in 1851 and rebuilt in 1912 with a mention of the foundation of the Halsall Girls' School founded in 1758. Moving on a decade, we find the Gothic-style terrace, Treleaven House, dated 1867. By the 1880s, the great building boom in terraces in the north end of Waterloo was underway. Numbers 5 and 7 Somerville Terrace are dated 1886 and 24 to 31 are dated 1887. The former police station in Seaforth Road has a fine moulded brick inscription including its

The stone plaque in St Luke's Halsall School, Cooks Road, gives a potted history of the school from 1758: money left by Catherine Halsall to establish a girls' school; to a new building in 1851 and a further rebuilding in 1912.

date, 1895. The progress of development is most clearly seen in South Road. From the railway station down to the shore, the buildings are much smaller and older with few exceptions built before the 1890s. Inland from the station, the date stones on the buildings show how South Road developed in the 1890s and early 1900s. On the north side, the block between Curzon Road and Willoughby Road has a plaque marking the opening of the Constitutional Club by the Honourable George Curzon in 1894. Curzon (1859-1925) was a local MP and a rising Conservative who was already serving as Under Secretary for India and who went on to become Viceroy of India. The Club was on the first floor and had a grand entrance on the corner of Curzon Road. On the opposite side of South Road there are three other blocks of shops, which are dated 1896, 1898 and 1903. There are similar blocks of three-storey shops in St John's Road dated 1897 and on College Road on the corner of Rossett Road dated 1903 and Moor Buildings, next to the George in Great Crosby village, also of 1903.

Some houses from the same period are also dated. Florence Terrace on Coronation Road opposite the park is dated 1899. This was when the road was still Thorpes Lane. Incidentally, there is also the question as to when its name was changed from Harps Lane as marked on the 1850 Ordnance Survey map. At the top of Kimberley Drive next to Liverpool Road, one house has a plaque in its gable dated 1899 while towards the other end there is another dated 1903. Numbers 35 to 37 Brooke Road West have a brick plaque dated 1901, and numbers 1 to 3 Princes Road off Coronation Road are dated 1903. 'Brooklyn' on Hall Road West is dated 1908 on a rainwater head. I am sure there are others to be spotted.

There are many datestones to be found on local houses. The first on a pair of houses in Vale Road, originally Alma Vale, is one of the earliest. At the Victoria Road end of Cambridge Road, Great Crosby, there is a pair of semi-detached houses which also share a datestone in a different style. Both houses have acquired later wall treatments such as pebble-dashing, which have changed their character.

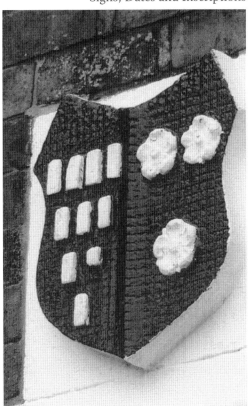

Heraldic emblems and signs document the importance of the Blundell family. This shield is to be found on a mock-Tudor house of 1866 next to Blundellsands station.

The fashion for date stones on public buildings and houses seems to have declined after 1910. The next ones I spotted were the Palladium cinema built in 1913 in Seaforth Road and the Bethel chapel in Seafield Avenue of 1914. Then there is a gap until the rebuilding of the Roman Catholic primary school on Liverpool Road, which is now the Chestnuts School, which was rebuilt in 1927. This is followed by the bold monogram and '1936' on the shops on the south side of Moor Lane. There is then nothing until the telephone exchange on Crosby Road North dated 1952 with George VI's monogram and a block of flats at the Moor Lane roundabout dated 1959. More recently, there has been a revival with two sets of shops in Liverpool Road, Crosby village, dated 1982 and 1992 and various housing developments such as Ramleh Close (built on the site of Sir William Forwood's house of that name) on Burbo Bank Road dated 1994, number 5 Walmer Road, Waterloo, 2002 and the flats that have replaced Alexandra Hall, 2004.

Another place to investigate local history through inscriptions is churchyards: the Anglican St Luke's and the Catholic St Peter and St Paul's in Great Crosby, St Mary's at Little Crosby and St Helen's at Sefton. The latter's churchyard is a reminder of Thomas Gray's famous poem, 'An Elegy in a Country Churchyard', and the lines:

Beneath those rugged elms, the yew tree's shade
Where heaves the turf in many a mouldering heap,
Each in his narrow cell for ever laid,
The rude forefathers of the hamlet sleep

Left: The Blundell's own house at Little Crosby is hidden away behind its own park wall, but no one can be left in any doubt of the standing of the family by the pair of heraldic lions at the hall's main entrance.

Opposite: A chance discovery in St Mary's churchyard, Little Crosby: Henry Norris lived to the very old age of 105 and was one of the first people to be buried there.

That is, if it were not for the smell of steak cooking in the kitchen of the Punchbowl Inn next door! As St Helen's was the only parish church in the whole district, it was the burying ground for the people of Great and Little Crosby, Waterloo, Ince Blundell, Litherland and Netherton until the mid-nineteenth century. The only exceptions were the Catholics buried in the Harkirk within the grounds of Little Crosby Hall. Most people had no memorial stone, but there are some in Sefton that date back to the seventeenth century such as that of Richard Pooley who died in 1676 and whose stone has been laid flat beside the main path to the church. It is rather crudely lettered compared with later ones. On the south side of the church close to the wall you can find the stones of William Catterall of Great Crosby (died 1824), William Yates of Waterloo (died 1839) and Thomas Hodson of Little Crosby (date obscured), and close to the vestry there is a stone commemorating the burial place of the poor of Ince Blundell. All these late eighteenth- and early nineteenth-century stones appear to be carved from local stones with distinctive curved, double curved or multiple curved tops and well-cut Roman font lettering. Later graves are of many different types of stone including a few in purple Welsh slate. I was drawn to one in particular which marks the burial place of Robert Davenport, 'thirteen years faithful servant of the adjoining rectory' who died in 1845, aged fifty-seven. He must have been a good servant to have deserved this. The rectors and the Molyneux and the Blundell families were buried in vaults below the church itself. The finest include the early fifteenth-century alabaster tomb of Johanna, wife of Sir Richard Molyneux, and the brass of another Sir Richard Molyneux and his family of 1558.

St Mary's, Little Crosby, has gravestones going back to about 1853. One that has been laid flat in front of the west tower records the burial place of Henry Norris who died in 1853, aged 105. The Blundells of Little Crosby have their own resting places marked by stone crosses near the chancel. That of Francis Nicholas Blundell who died in 1884 is especially elaborate with a rustic cross carrying a wreath, mounted on a rocky plinth covered in realistically carved ferns.

St Peter and St Paul's was established in 1826 and certainly had a burial ground by 1850 when it was shown on the Ordnance Survey map of that year. The earliest marked burial I could find was that of the Davies family from 1841. This was a large plinth surmounted by a cross, and there many other large memorials here. For example, there are many Celtic crosses as you might expect with so many local families originating from Ireland. The biggest commemorates the nuns of Mount Pleasant Convent who died between 1883 and 1898. Some have full-size statues of either Jesus or Our Lady. St Patrick, with his stick pinning down one of the snakes he banished from Ireland, tops the memorial to James Moran. He was the general secretary of the Irish National Foresters of England and Wales until he died in 1935. The Foresters were among the biggest of the friendly societies, which provided working-class people with a means of saving and paid out for sickness and deaths. As most extracted an oath of secrecy from their members, they could also be the cover for political activities, and as Irishmen were feared and despised in the nineteenth century, much as immigrants are today, it was not surprising they formed their own self-help organisations. This society certainly had nationalist intentions because the inscription reads:

Above: Sefton churchyard has many early nineteenth-century headstones which were probably made by local masons. They have a characteristic wavy top and simple but very elegant lettering.

Left: St Peter and St Paul's churchyard has some striking monuments, including this giant Celtic cross dedicated to the nuns of Mount Pleasant Convent.

Nearby, the life-size statue of St Patrick
was paid for by public subscription in
memory of the Irish patriot, James Moran.

The biggest and most idiosyncratic memorials
in St Luke's churchyard date back to the
Victorian era. Many of the carvings are very
intricate and this carved head seems to be
a portrait of Mary Fogg, 'relict' of Thomas
Fogg, who died in 1856.

The headstone of an unsung hero. Captain Strachan of Crosby gave away his lifebelt to a young stowaway when his ship, the steamer *Cyprian*, was wrecked off the coast of North Wales. His stone in front of St Luke's church is decorated with 'a fouled anchor' – an anchor with its chain wrapped its stock. This was a common motif for mariners' graves.

'A sterling patriot who was actively identified with every movement calculated to secure the freedom of his native land and the welfare of the Irish people' and his monument was paid for by public subscription.

Among the 4,000 graves of St Luke's churchyard are also some striking Victorian memorials. The first burial was that of the church's first vicar, the Revd Richard Walker, who had worked tirelessly to get his new church built and died within three months of its consecration. He is buried under a large horizontal stone immediately behind the church. Around him there is a splendid selection of obelisks, turrets and spires and broken columns. Many of these are large family vaults. Some of the names are unusual, including Trampleasure, Campbell Sweeney Lemon or Kruse Caroe, the father of the church architect W.D. Caroe, or Thomas Fogg whose Gothic monument appears to have portraits of the family at each corner.

There are many mariner's graves because Great Crosby and Waterloo were nautical enclaves. Among them is a single slate gravestone of George Bark, a Liverpool pilot who died in 1854 at the young age of thirty-one. Many of their graves are marked with carved anchors. One of the most interesting is that of Captain John Strachan which is situated to the right of the main entrance to the church. On 13 October 1881, he was master of the

Liverpool steamer *Cyprian* outward bound for the Mediterranean. The *Cyprian* was caught in a north-western gale and went to shelter in Caernarvon Bay. During the night she suffered a series of mechanical mishaps. First, a boiler broke down, then the steering gear, and then the second boiler. The storm was so fierce that both anchors failed to stop her being wrecked. When Captain Strachan ordered the crew to abandon ship on the afternoon of the next day, he noticed a young stowaway, called Khalan, who had abandoned his hide-out in one of the boats. Realising he had no lifejacket, he took his own off saying, 'Here you are, take mine, I'll swim for it'. These were his last words, for poor Captain Strachan was drowned. The twelve-year-old stowaway survived and later became the master of a ship. Captain Strachan's body was brought back to Great Crosby for burial where he had lived with his parents at Holly Hedge, Moor Lane. There is another *Cyprian* connection in that number 17 Kingsway is named Cyprian Villa (carved into the gateposts). As this house was built sometime between 1920 and 1925 and was occupied by Mr Arthur Lewis, it is difficult to see any connection with the wrecked *Cyprian*. Perhaps the house was named after another Leyland Line ship because all their ships' names ended in 'ian'.

These are only a few examples of what you can see on local buildings and in local churchyards. Perhaps, though, the most poignant of all inscriptions are the long lists of names carved on our local war memorials: the extent of the losses, especially in the First World War, was horrendous.

In praise of Waterloo from the *Seaside Tatler*, 1860.

But I seek thy smiling shore,
Where in mazy circle soar,
Albatross and wild sea-mew,
Waterloo!

Then before me schooners, brigs,
Steamers, sloops – all sorts of rigs,
Pass in panoramic view
Waterloo!

While in nearer prospect seen,
Gorgeous groups of crinoline,
Spiflicate me through and through,
Waterloo!

Bibliography

Ackroyd, H., *Picture Palaces of Liverpool*, Liverpool, 2002

Anon. *Local Maps and Documents in the Local History Library* (2nd edition), Crosby, 1972

Blundell, M., *A Lancashire Squire: The Life of Nicholas Blundell of Crosby 1669-1737*, reprinted at Crowborough, 2002

Connolly, A., *Life in the Victorian Brickyards of Flintshire and Denbighshire*, Llanrwst, 2003

Cochrane, J., *Mills, Mollies and Marl Pits: The Story of the Township of Great Crosby*, Crosby, 2005

Alan Godfrey Maps of Blundellsands and Great Crosby 1907 and Waterloo with Seaforth 1925

Greenwood, E.F. (ed.), *Ecology and Landscape A History of the Mersey Basin*, London, 1999

Hamilton-Fazey, I., 'Waterloo Rugby Football Club: An Historical Perspective' on www.waterloorugby.com

Harrop, S., *Merchant Taylor's School for Girls*, Liverpool, 1988

Heath, T., *Crosby, Seaforth and Waterloo*, Stroud, 2000

Heath, T., *Crosby, Seaforth and Waterloo: The Second Selection*, Stroud, 2001

Hollinghurst, H., (ed.), *St Luke's Church, Great Crosby, 1853-2003*, Crosby, 2003

Hollinghurst, H. with Gill, J., *St Michael's Church: A Centenary History*, Blundellsands, 2005

Hull, R.C., 'Social Differentiation in a North Liverpool Suburb. The Case of Great Crosby and Waterloo 1841-1901', MA thesis, University of Liverpool. There is a copy in Crosby Local History Library

Jarvis, R.C., (ed.), 'Customs Letter-books of the Port of Liverpool 1711-1813', *Chetham Society* vol. 6 (third series), letter 204

Lewis, J., 'Sefton's Rural Fringes' in *The Archaeology of a Changing Landscape. The last 1,000 Years in Merseyside*, Merseyside Archaeological Society vol. 11, 2002

Lewis, J.R., *The Birth of Waterloo* (3rd edition), Southport, 1996

Luft, H.M., *The History of Merchant Taylor's School, Crosby*, Liverpool, 1970

Maddock, A., 'Watercourse management and flood prevention in the Alt Level, Lancashire, 1589-1779' in *The Transactions of the Lancashire and Cheshire Historic Society*, vol. 148 (1999), pp 59-94

Matthews, J. and Davidson, F.B., *History of Waterloo Park Cricket Club 1890-1950*, Waterloo, 1950

Miller, J.A., *A Bibliography of Crosby and District*, Crosby, 1974

Pevsner, N., *Buildings of England, Lancashire the Industrial and Commercial South*, London, 1969

Pinkman, J.A., (Maguire, F.E. ed.), *In the Legion of the Vanguard*, Boulder, Colorado, 1999. (Reminiscences of IRA activity before the Second World War)

Price, D. *The Northern Cricket Club 1859-1961*, Crosby, 1985

Rothwell, M., *A Guide to the Industrial Heritage of Accrington*, Accrington, 1979

Smith, J.T., 'Timber-framed buildings in England' in *The Archaeological Journal* Vol. 122 (1965), pp 132-158

Stanistreet, J.E., and Farthing, A., *Crosby in Camera: Early Photographs of Great Crosby and Waterloo*, Southport, 1995

Stanistreet, J.E., Sargant, M.J. and Lee-Hart, A., *Seaforth in Camera*, Southport, 1999

Tyrer, F., *Let's Walk to Little Crosby*, Southport, 1992

Tyrer, F., *The Windmills of Crosby*, Crosby, 1972

Woods, E.C., 'Some history of the coastwise lights of Lancashire and Cheshire' in *Transactions of the Lancashire and Cheshire Historic Society* vols 96-98, 81-103, 159-80 and 107-12

Wotherspoon, D., *The Mighty Mariners*, Downholland, 1997

Index

Other local titles published by Tempus

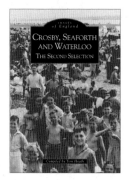

Crosby, Seaforth and Waterloo: Second Selection
TOM HEATH

In this book, Tom Heath's second selection of old images in this series, he again takes readers on a nostalgic tour of the old Merseyside communities of Crosby, Waterloo, Blundellsands, Seaforth and Litherland. Most of the 200 photographs in the book were taken by Crosby photographer Stephen Cushing who died in 1937 and had a studio and shop in Moor Lane, Crosby for thirty years.

0-7524-2440-8

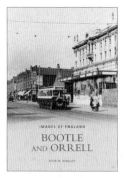

Bootle and Orrell
PETER W. WOOLLEY

Illustrated with over 200 old photographs and picture postcards dating from 1896 to the present day, this book aims to provide a guided tour around some of the main streets in Bootle and Orrell. Particular attention is paid to the May blitz during the Second World War which devastated Bootle, while everyday life is also featured, from schools and churches, shops and industry, to sporting events, leisure pursuits and, of course, the local townspeople.

0-7524-3360-1

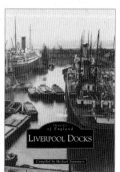

Liverpool Docks
MICHAEL STAMMERS

The story of Liverpool is, in many ways, the story of its docks. With contemporary illustrations of people, ships, buildings and machinery, Michael Stammers chronicles not just the rise and fall of Mersey shipping but also the way the docks have bounced back. Redevelopment, restoration and new modes of commerce have put Liverpool's docks back in the black, albeit looking very different to the port of sixty years ago.

0-7524-1712-6

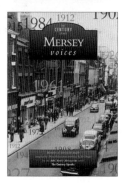

Mersey Voices
DIANA PULSON AND EV DRAPER

This collection of reminiscences of Merseyside's people was selected by Diana Pulson from interviews recorded by Ev Draper for a series of local radio programmes to mark the Millennium, called The Century Speaks. The memories – illustrated with contemporary photographs – describe days long gone, the continual struggle to get by, events both comic and tragic and are a fitting reminder of how we lived in the twentieth century.

0-7524-1835-1

If you are interested in purchasing other books published by Tempus, or in case you have difficulty finding any Tempus books in your local bookshop, you can also place orders directly through our website

www.tempus-publishing.com